ABOUT KUMON

KUM⊙N®
MATH. READING. SUCCESS.

What is Kumon?

Kumon is the world's largest supplemental education provider and a leader in producing outstanding results. After-school programs in math and reading at Kumon Centers around the globe have been helping children succeed for 50 years.

Kumon Workbooks represent just a fraction of our complete curriculum of preschool-to-college-level material assigned at Kumon Centers under the supervision of trained Kumon Instructors.

The Kumon Method enables each child to progress successfully by practicing material until concepts are mastered and advancing in small, manageable increments. Instructors carefully assign materials and pace advancement according to the strengths and needs of each individual student.

Students usually attend a Kumon Center twice a week and practice at home the other five days. Assignments take about twenty minutes.

Kumon helps students of all ages and abilities master the basics, improve concentration and study habits, and build confidence.

How did Kumon begin?

IT ALL BEGAN IN JAPAN 50 YEARS AGO when a parent and teacher named Toru Kumon found a way to help his son Takeshi do better in school. At the prompting of his wife, he created a series of short assignments that his son could complete successfully in less than 20 minutes a day and that would ultimately make high school math easy. Because each was just a bit more challenging than the last, Takeshi was able to master the skills and gain the confidence to keep advancing.

This unique self-learning method was so successful that Toru's son was able to do calculus by the time he was in the sixth grade. Understanding the value of good reading comprehension, Mr. Kumon then developed a reading program employing the same method. His programs are the basis and inspiration of those offered at Kumon Centers today under the expert guidance of professional Kumon Instructors.

Mr. Toru Kumon
Founder of Kumon

What can Kumon do for my child?

Kumon is geared to children of all ages and skill levels. Whether you want to give your child a leg up in his or her schooling, build a strong foundation for future studies or address a possible learning problem, Kumon provides an effective program for developing key learning skills given the strengths and needs of each individual child.

What makes Kumon so different?

Kumon uses neither a classroom model nor a tutoring approach. It's designed to facilitate self-acquisition of the skills and study habits needed to improve academic performance. This empowers children to succeed on their own, giving them a sense of accomplishment that fosters further achievement. Whether for remedial work or enrichment, a child advances according to individual ability and initiative to reach his or her full potential. Kumon is not only effective, but also surprisingly affordable.

What is the role of the Kumon Instructor?

Kumon Instructors regard themselves more as mentors or coaches than teachers in the traditional sense. Their principal role is to provide the direction, support and encouragement that will guide the student to performing at 100% of his or her potential. Along with their rigorous training in the Kumon Method, all Kumon Instructors share a passion for education and an earnest desire to help children succeed.

KUMON FOSTERS:

- A mastery of the basics of reading and math
- Improved concentration and study habits
- Increased self-discipline and self-confidence
- A proficiency in material at every level
- Performance to each student's full potential
- A sense of accomplishment

▶▶ GETTING STARTED IS EASY. Just call us at 877.586.6671 or visit kumon.com to request our free brochure and find a Kumon Center near you. We'll direct you to an Instructor who will be happy to speak with you about how Kumon can address your child's particular needs and arrange a free placement test. There are more than 1,700 Kumon Centers in the U.S. and Canada, and students may enroll at any time throughout the year, even summer. Contact us today.

FIND OUT MORE ABOUT KUMON MATH & READING CENTERS.
Receive a free copy of our parent guide, *Every Child an Achiever,* by visiting
kumon.com/go.survey or calling **877.586.6671**

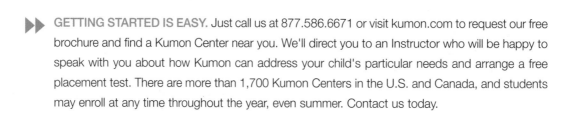

Let's Eat!

Name

Date

To parents Enjoyable connect-the-dots activities are on odd-numbered pages. It is okay if your child draws shaky lines at first; his or her fine motor skills will improve. Ask your child to guess what is shown in the picture. (The answers are at the end of this book.) For extra fun, your child can also color the pictures.

■ Draw a line from 1 to 10 in order while saying each number.

What Is It?

To parents On even-numbered pages are color-by-number activities. If your child has difficulty finding the numbers, please point them out. Praise your child as he or she finishes each activity.

■ Use the key below to color by number.
　I = yellow

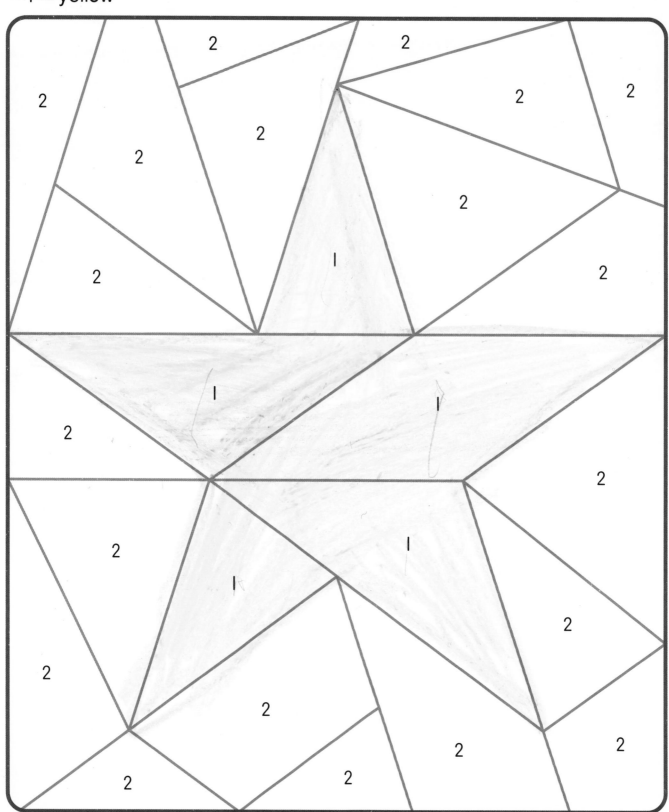

My Own Place

■ Draw a line from 1 to 10 in order while saying each number.

What Is It?

■ Use the key below to color by number.
  3 = brown   4 = orange

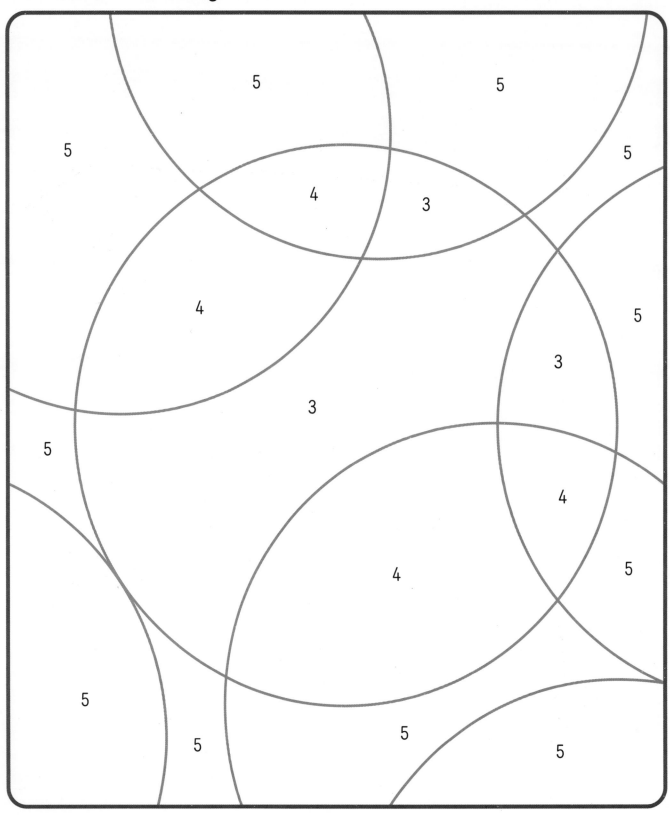

4

I Can Fly Fast!

■ Draw a line from 1 to 10 in order while saying each number.

What Is It?

■ Use the key below to color by number.
6 = green   7 = yellow

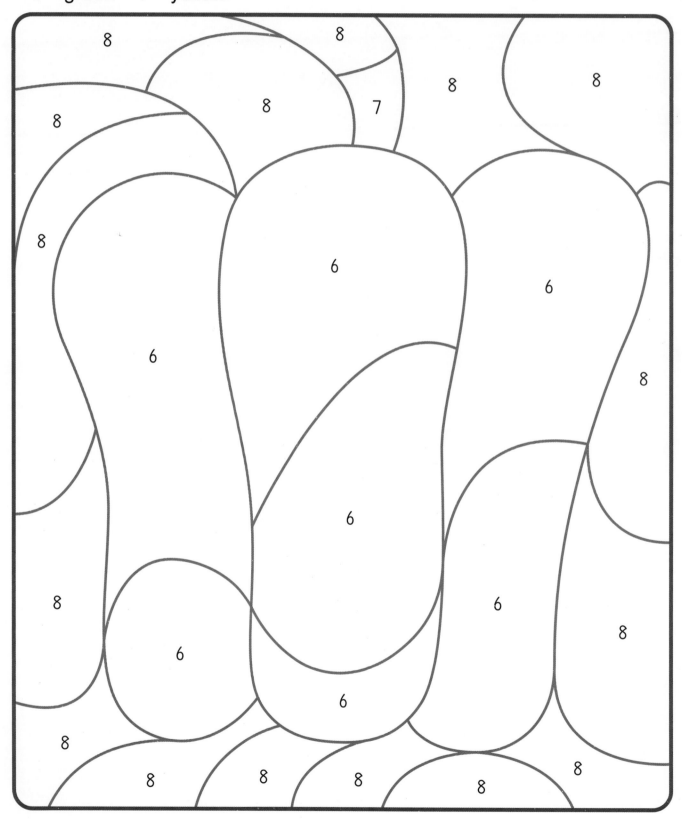

Ka-boom!

■ Draw a line from 1 to 15 in order while saying each number.

What Is It?

■ Use the key below to color by number.
   11 = brown   12 = yellow

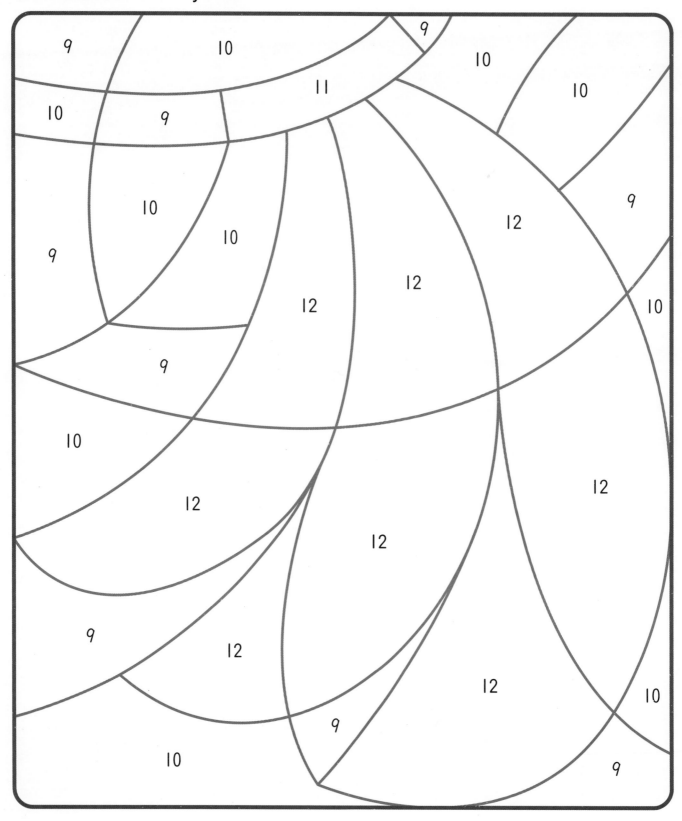

Whoosh

Name

Date

To parents On this page, your child will have to draw a line that will cross another line. If your child has difficulty finding the next number, please point it out for him or her. Please praise your child as he or she finishes each activity.

■ Draw a line from 1 to 15 in order while saying each number.

What Is It?

■ Use the key below to color by number.
13 = brown   14 = orange

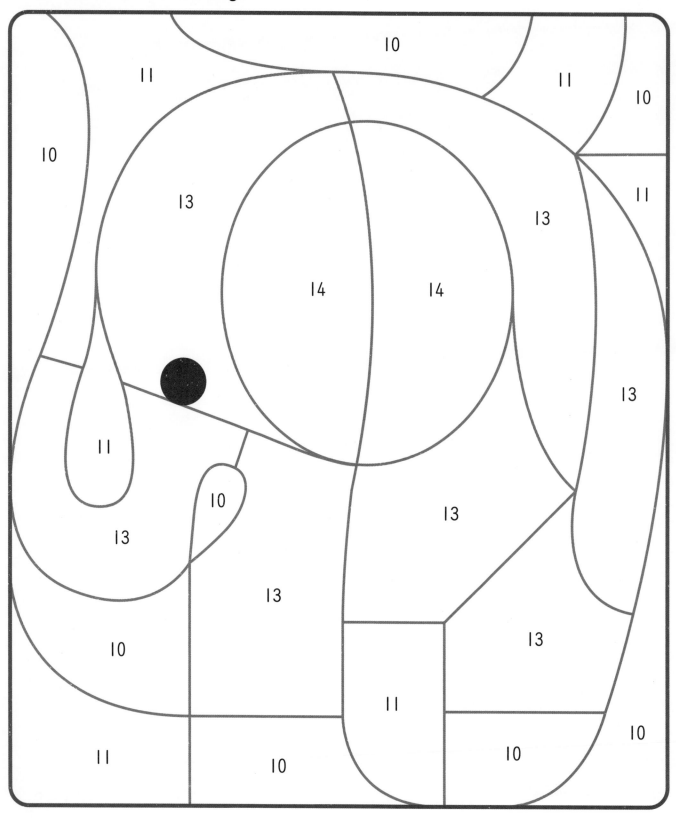

6 I Like to Camp

Name

Date

■ Draw a line from I to I5 in order while saying each number.

11

What Is It?

■ Use the key below to color by number.
14 = orange   15 = red

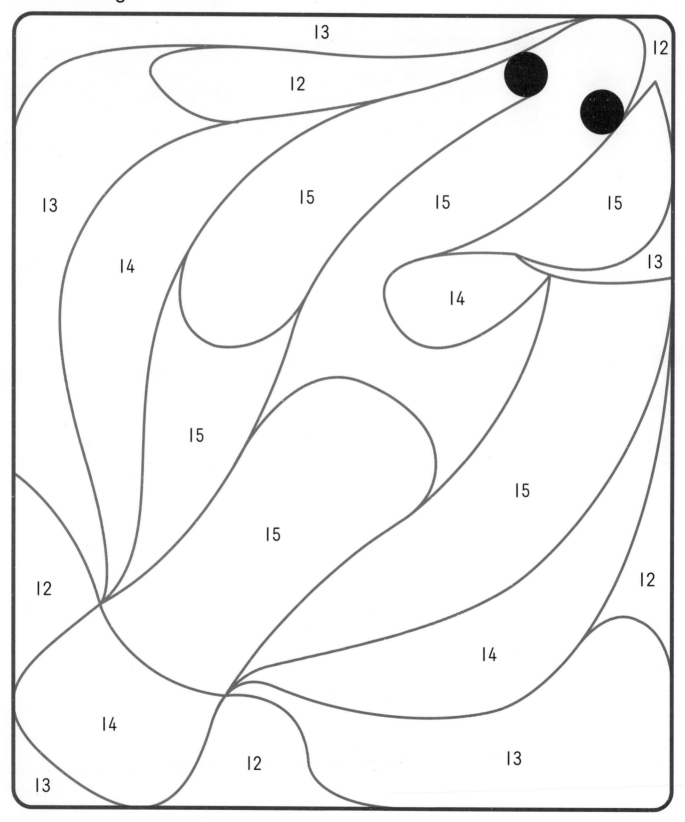

Happy Holidays!

Name

Date

■ Draw a line from 1 to 20 in order while saying each number.

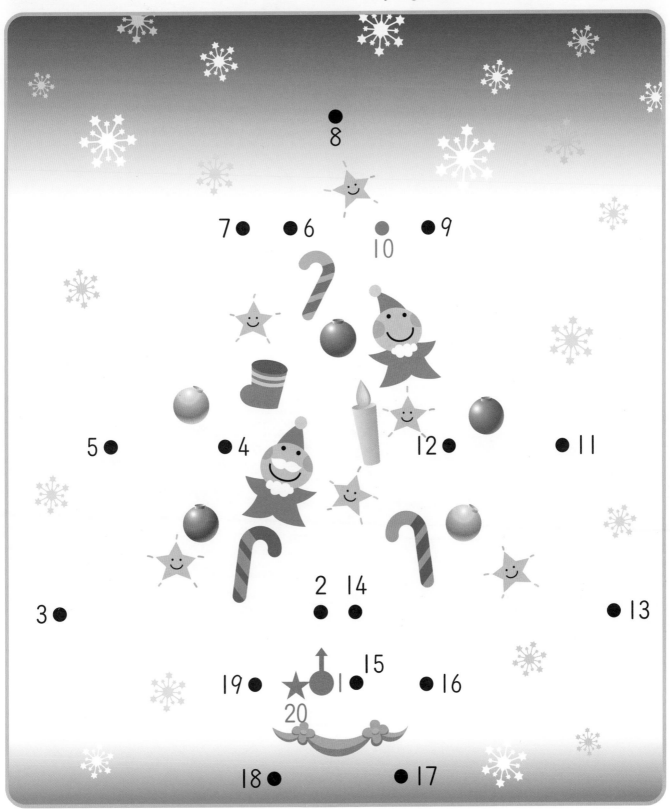

What Is It?

■ Use the key below to color by number.
16 = blue   17 = red

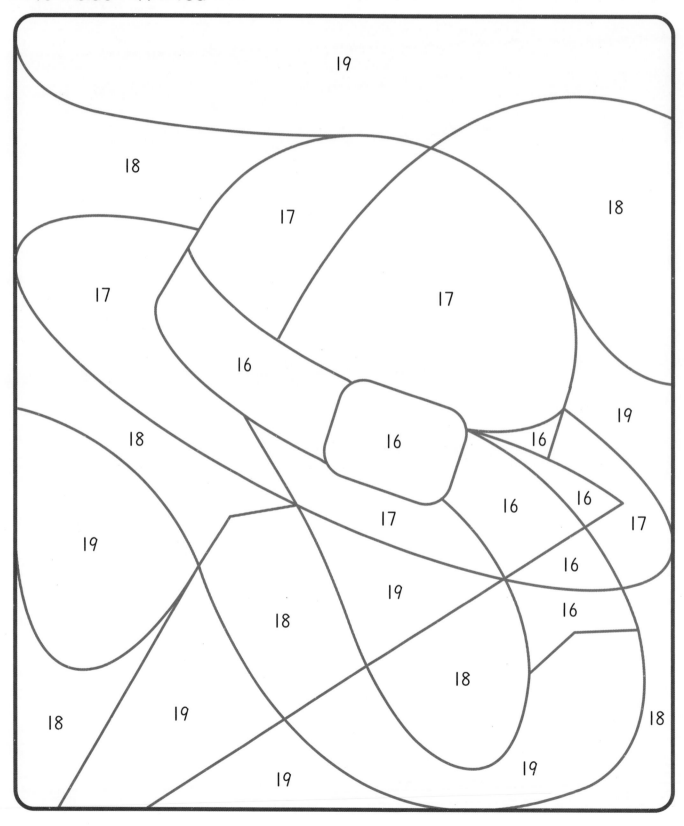

 **I Like Rainy Days**

■ Draw a line from I to 20 in order while saying each number.

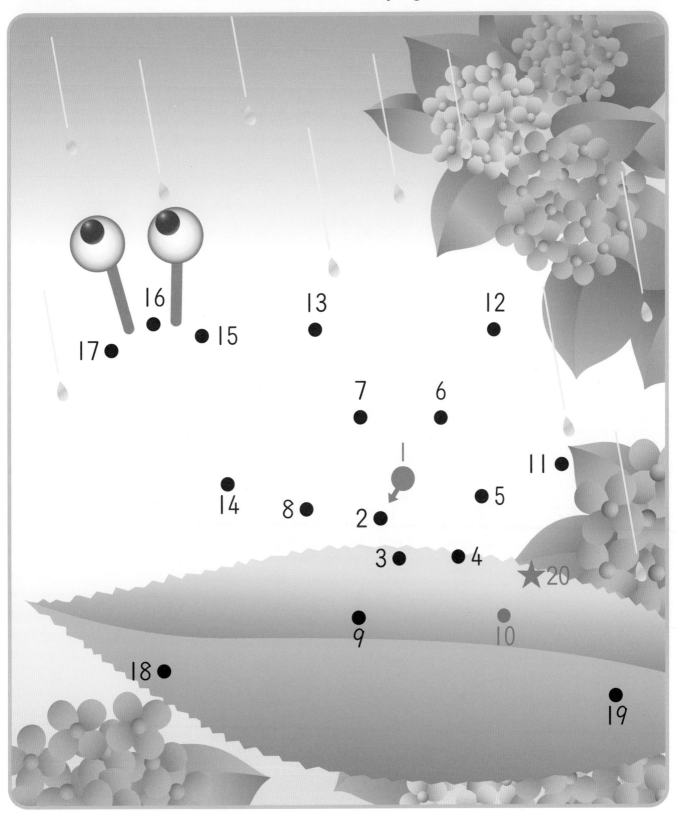

What Is It?

■ Use the key below to color by number.
   18 = brown   19 = yellow

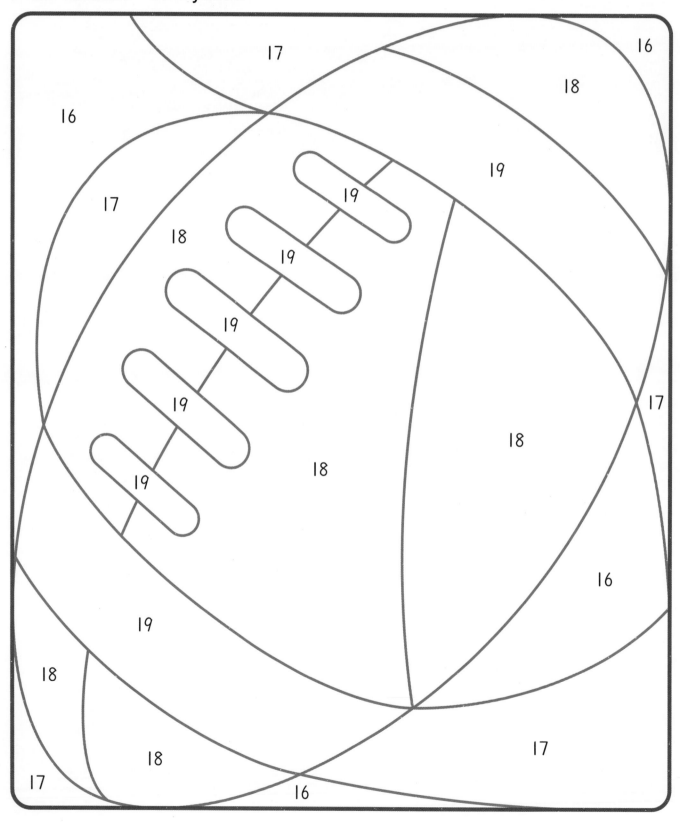

16

I Love Flowers

Name

Date

To parents Starting on page 17, there are several points where children must draw a line that will cross another line. If your child has difficulty finding the numbers, please point them out for him or her. Please praise your child as he or she finishes each activity.

■ Draw a line from 1 to 20 in order while saying each number.

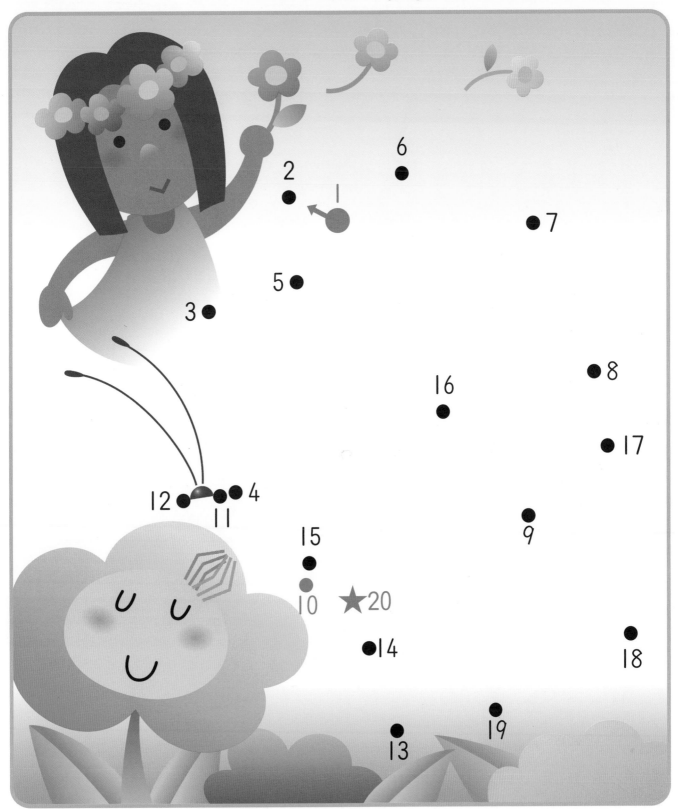

What Is It?

■ Use the key below to color by number.
   19 = green   20 = brown

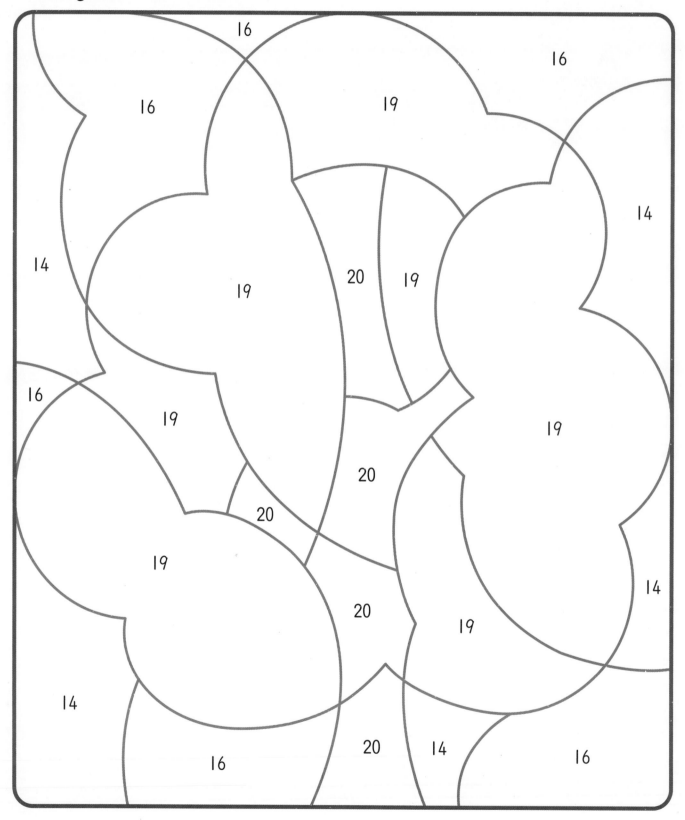

10 In the Forest

■ Draw a line from 1 to 30 in order while saying each number.

What Is It?

■ Use the key below to color by number.

21 = yellow   22 = green

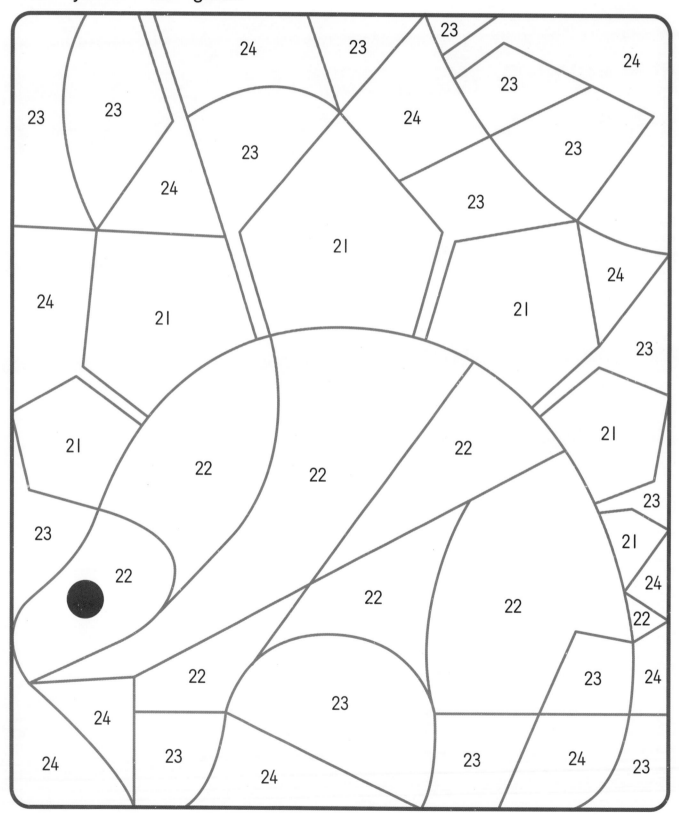

Is It a Beautiful Flower?

Name

Date

■ Draw a line from I to 30 in order while saying each number.

What Is It?

■ Use the key below to color by number.
   23 = yellow   24 = black

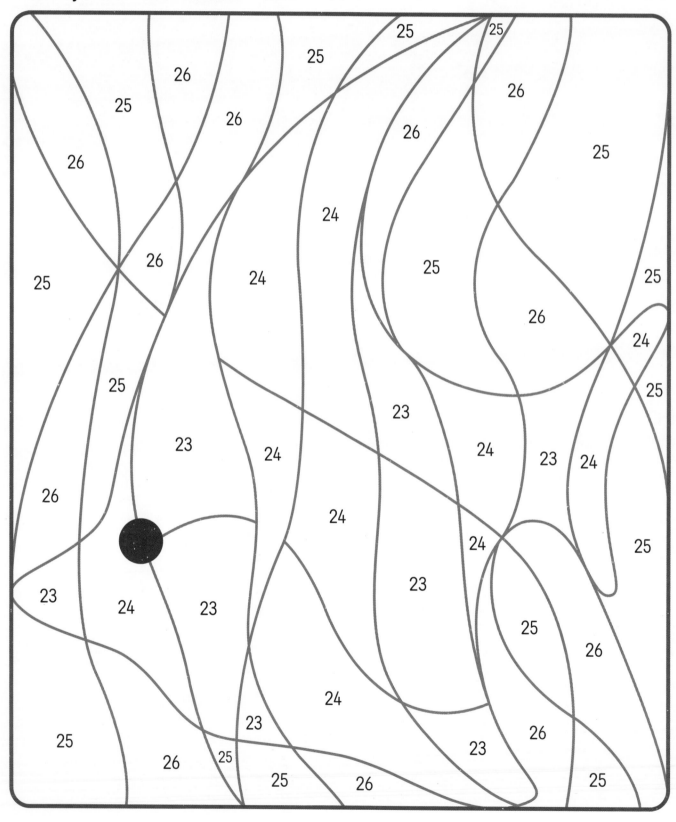

22

Who Is Playing with the Ball?

Name

Date

■ Draw a line from 1 to 30 in order while saying each number.

What Is It?

■ Use the key below to color by number.
26 = yellow   27 = blue

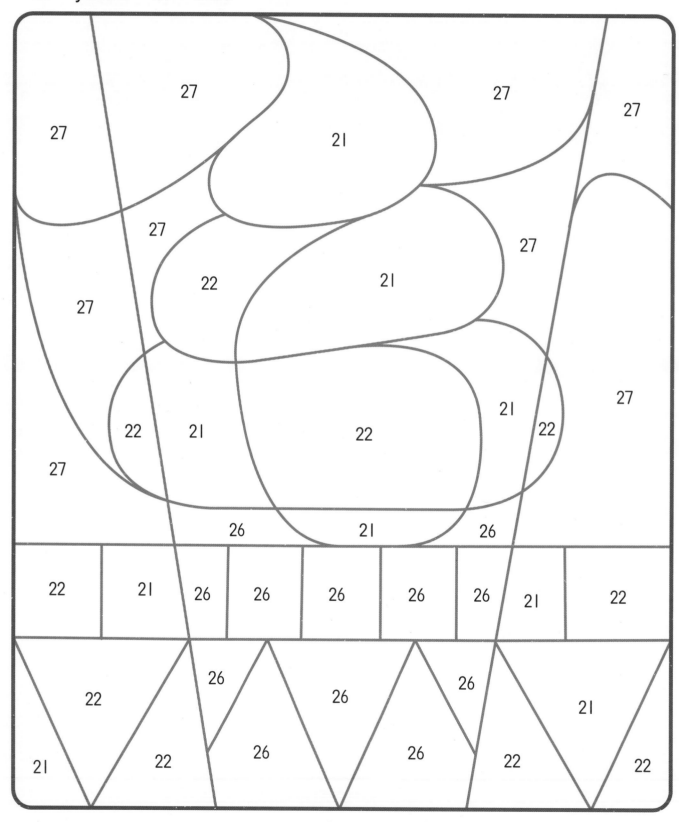

Name

Date

■ Draw a line from 1 to 30 in order while saying each number.

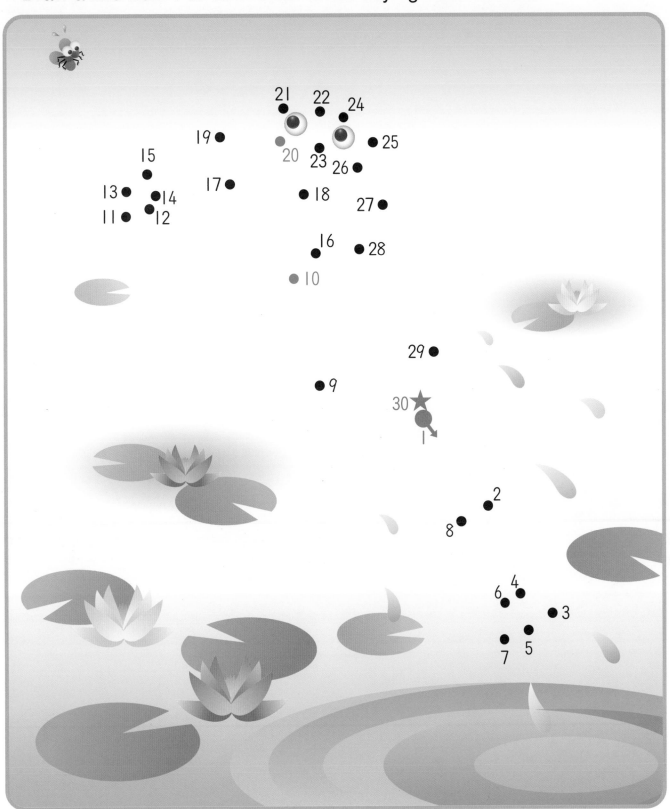

25

What Is It?

- Use the key below to color by number.
  28 = brown   29 = blue   30 = green

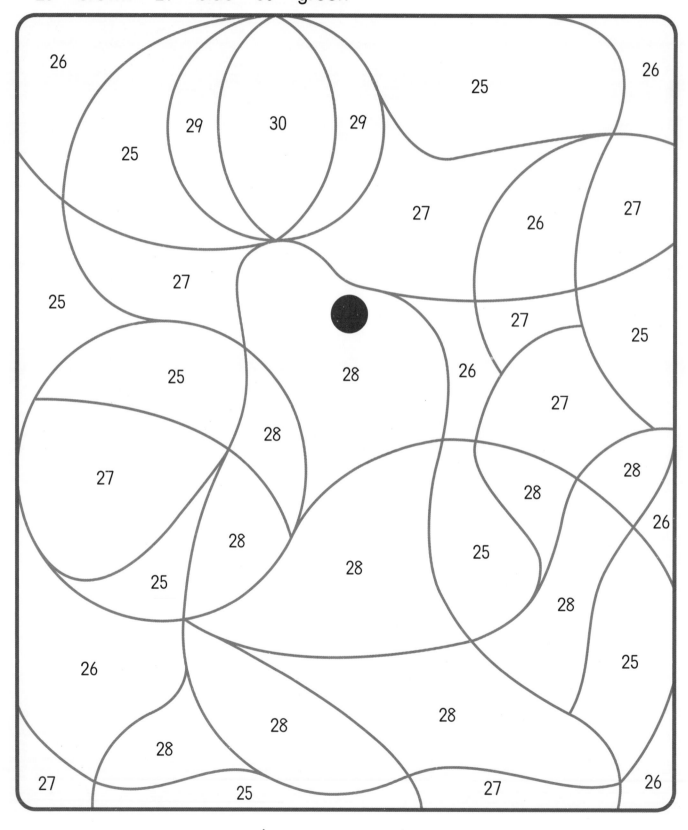

26

■ Draw a line from I to 30 in order while saying each number.

What Is It?

■ Use the key below to color by number.
21 = blue   22 = green   23 = yellow

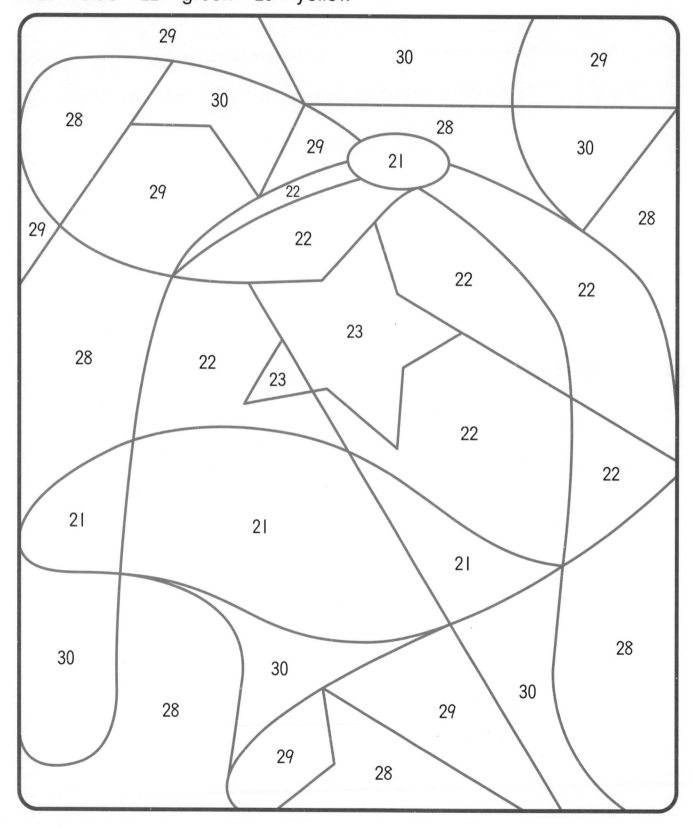

15 Up, Up, and Away!

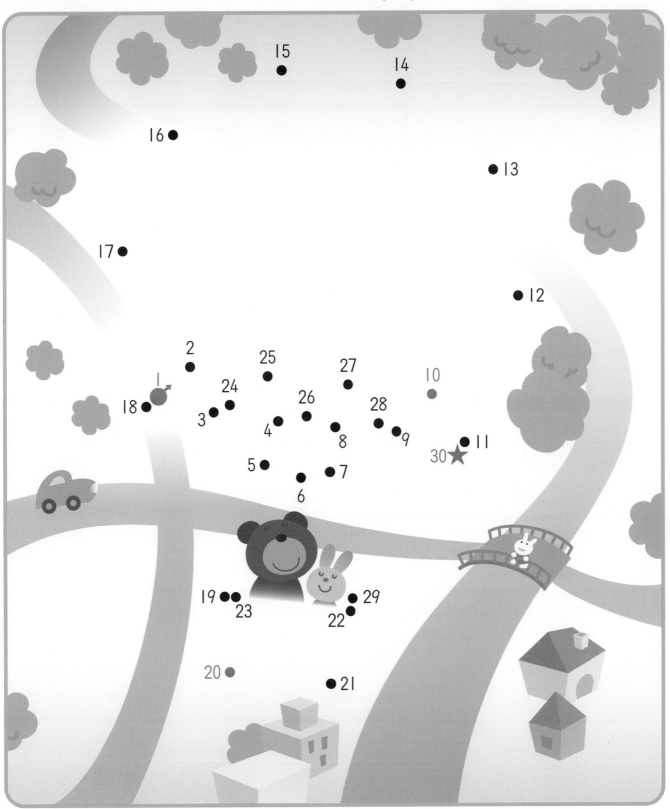

■ Draw a line from 1 to 30 in order while saying each number.

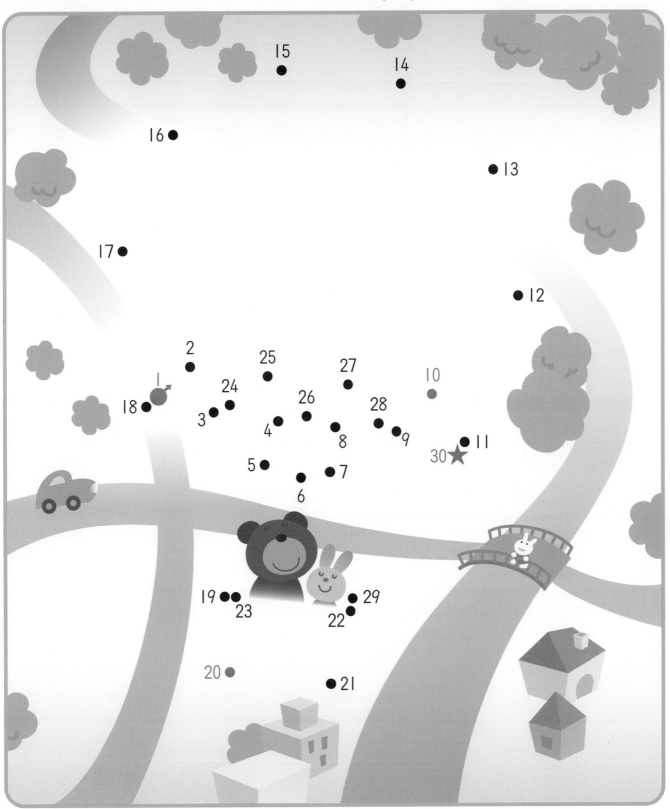

What Is It?

■ Use the key below to color by number.
25 = blue   26 = orange   27 = yellow

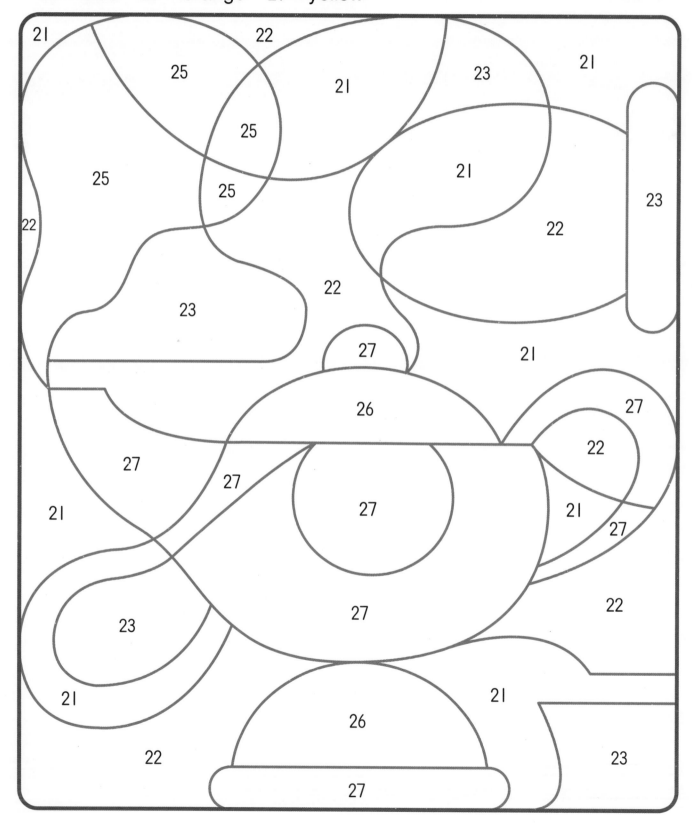

30

16 Is It a Big Bubble Bath?

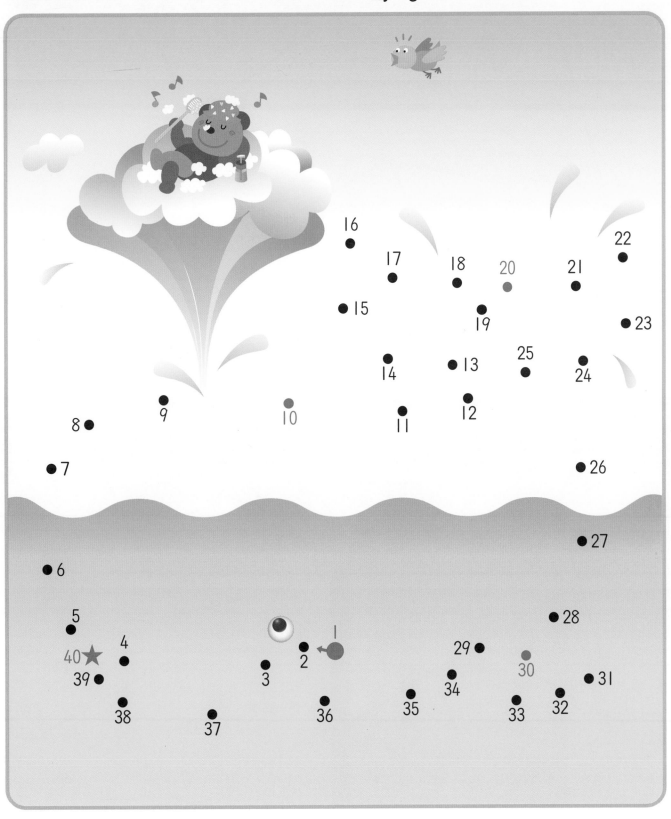

■ Draw a line from 1 to 40 in order while saying each number.

What Is It?

■ Use the key below to color by number.
31 = red   32 = orange   33 = green

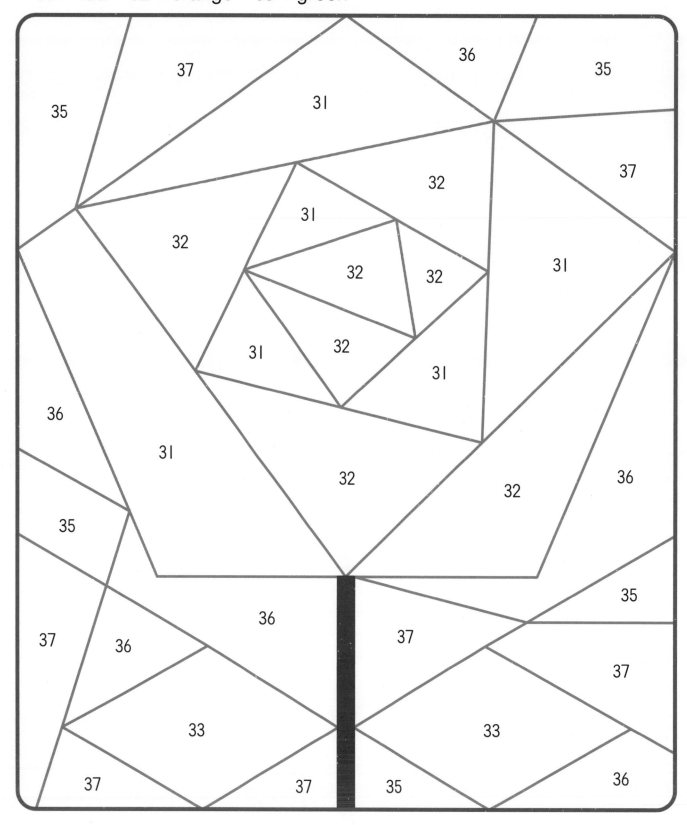

32

■ Draw a line from 1 to 40 in order while saying each number.

17

16

18

30

27

19

28

25

29

26

15

33

31

24

32

34

20

35

21

14

11

23

1

36

38

22

10

37

40

13   12

39

9

2

6   5

8   7

4   3

What Is It?

■ Use the key below to color by number.
33 = red   34 = orange   35 = green

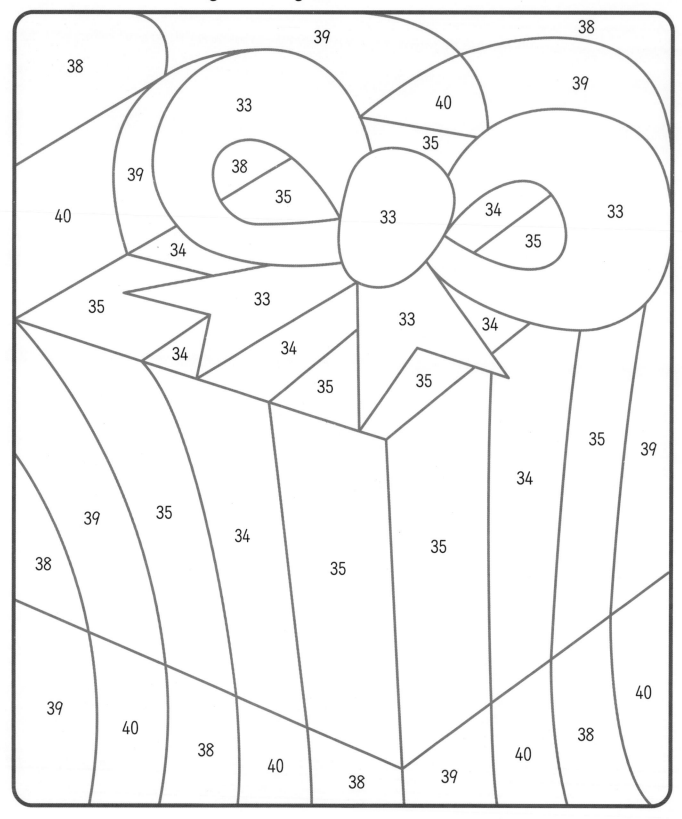

34

18 Moonlight Music

Name

Date

■ Draw a line from 1 to 40 in order while saying each number.

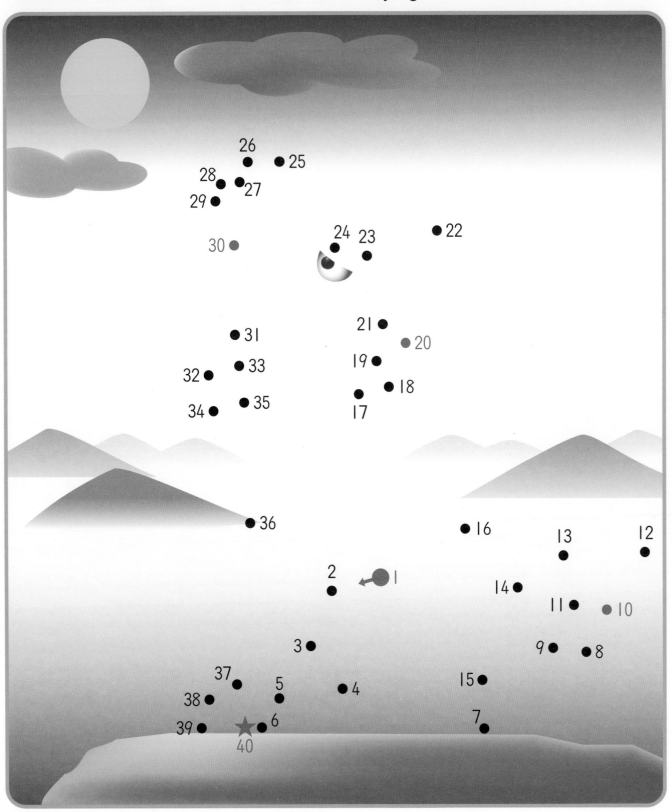

What Is It?

■ Use the key below to color by number.
36 = red   37 = yellow   38 = orange

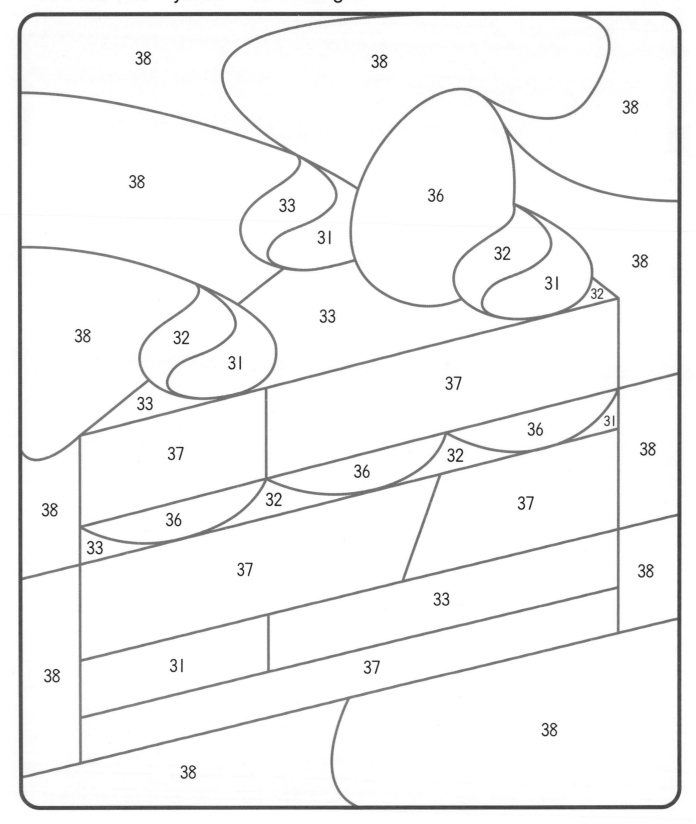

I Love These Leaves!

Name

Date

■ Draw a line from 1 to 40 in order while saying each number.

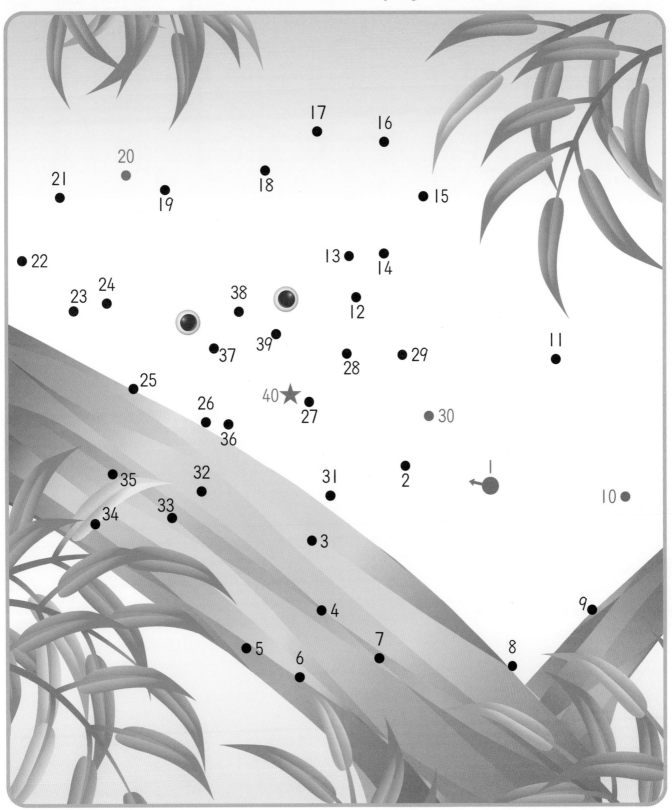

What Is It?

■ Use the key below to color by number.
38 = yellow   39 = green   40 = red

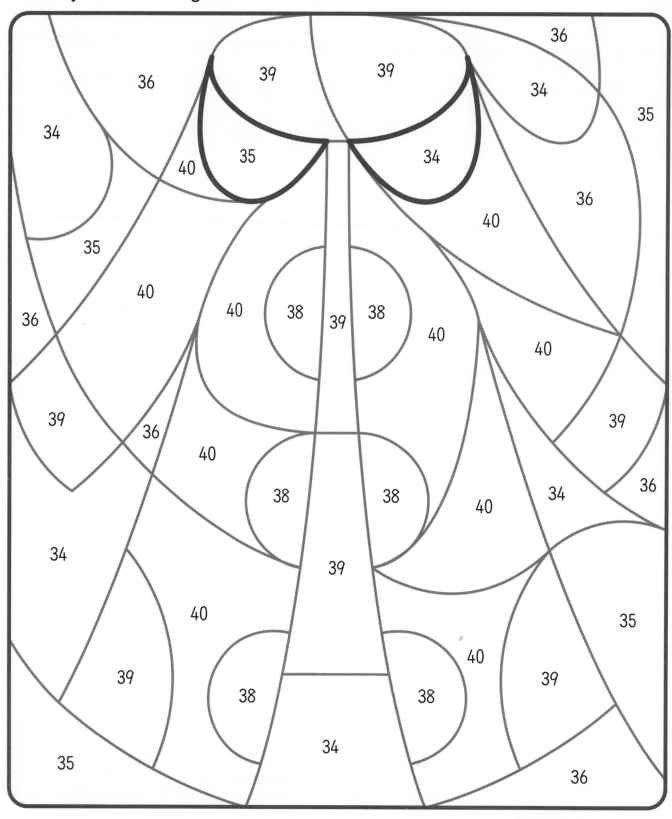

38

20 What a Catch!

■ Draw a line from 1 to 40 in order while saying each number.

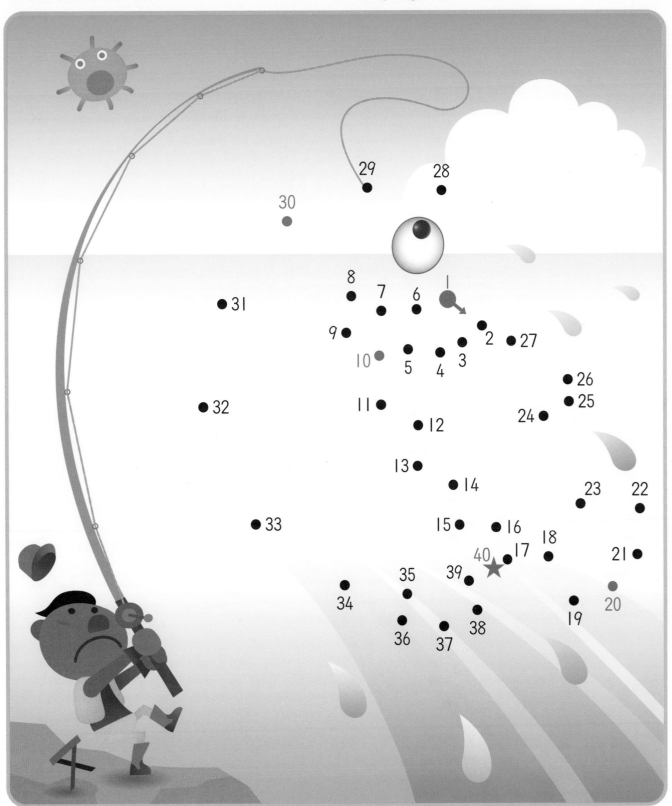

What Is It?

■ Use the key below to color by number.
   31 = black   34 = orange   36 = yellow

At the Circus

Name	
Date	

■ Draw a line from 1 to 40 in order while saying each number.

What Is It?

■ Use the key below to color by number.
  32 = orange   35 = red   39 = yellow   40 = blue

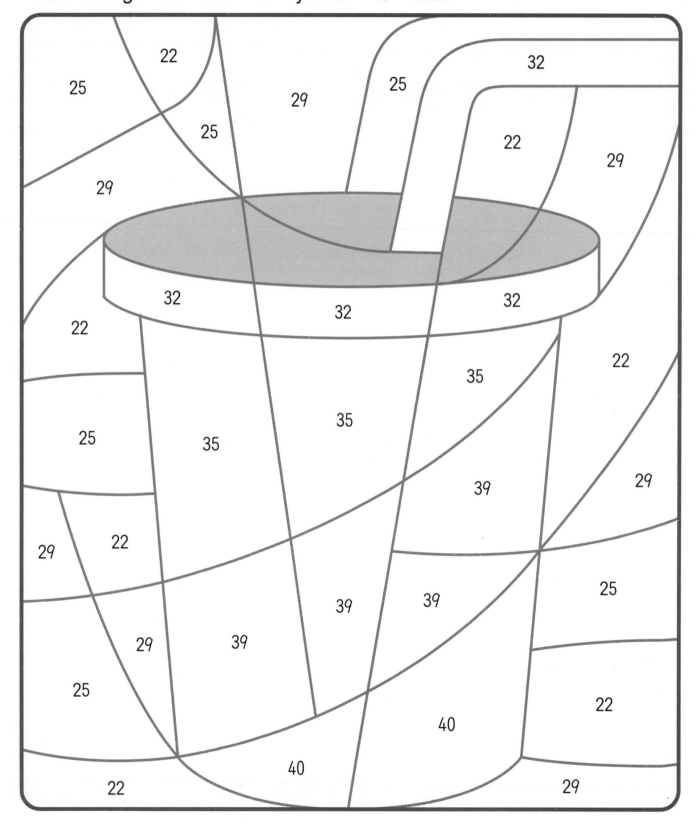

Hello

■ Draw a line from 1 to 40 in order while saying each number.

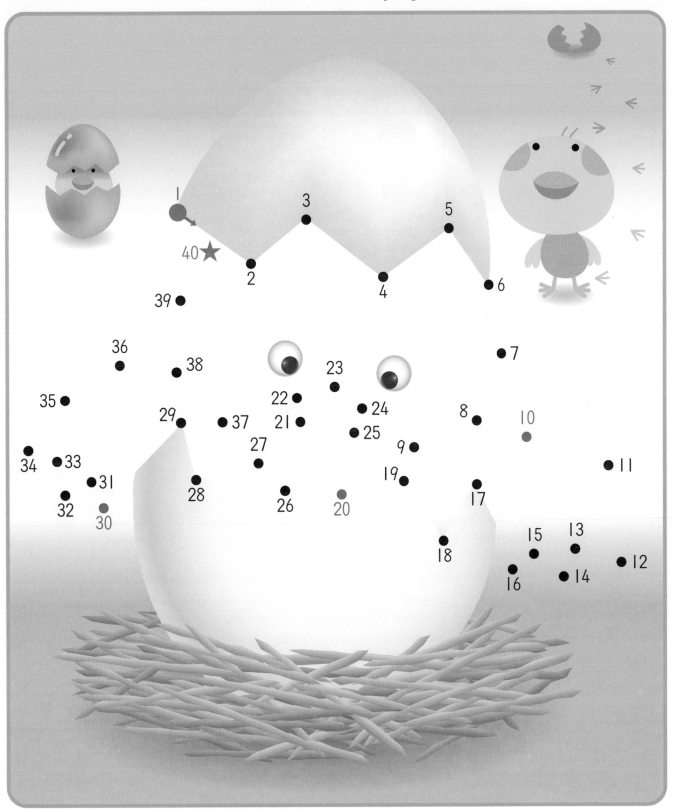

43

What Is It?

■ Use the key below to color by number.
33 = yellow   37 = red   38 = violet (purple)   40 = brown

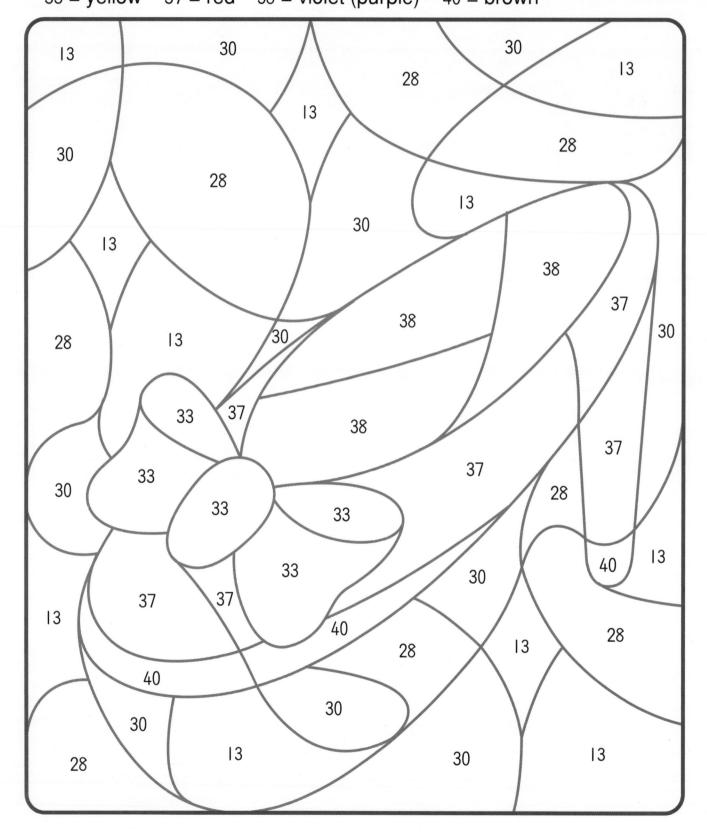

44

23 What Is in the Egg?

Name

Date

■ Draw a line from 1 to 50 in order while saying each number.

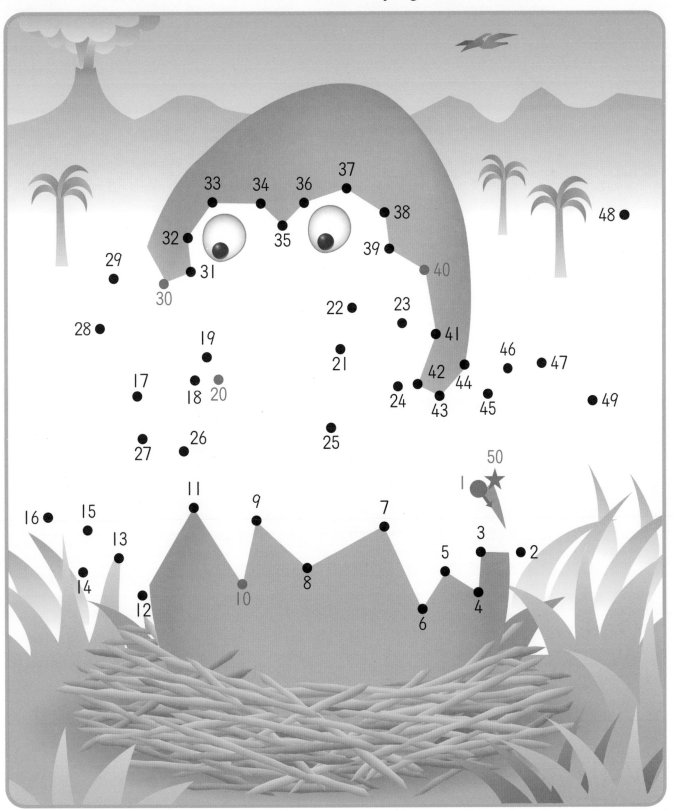

What Is It?

■ Use the key below to color by number.
41 = yellow   42 = blue   43 = black   44 = green

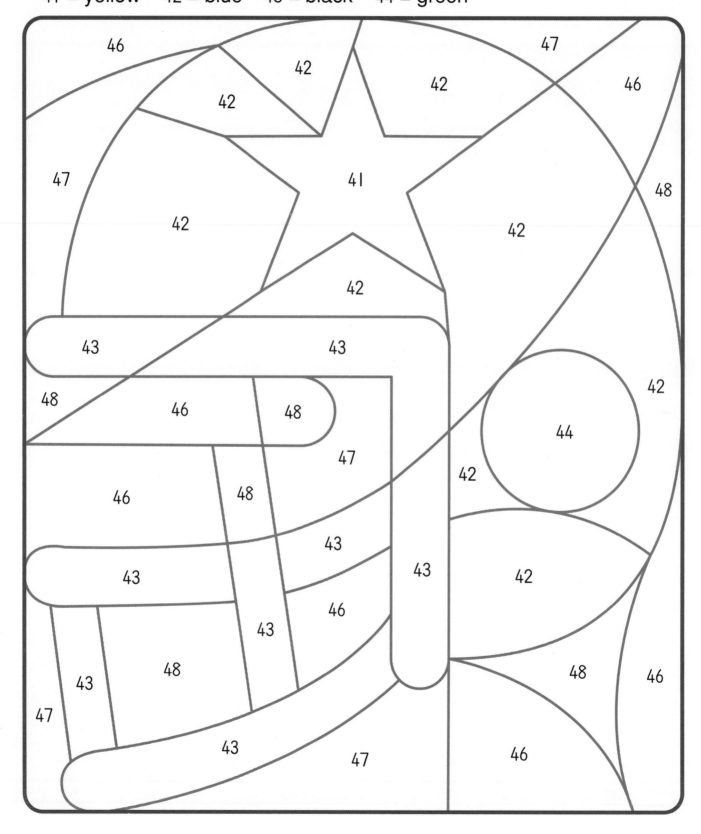

46

In Mommy's Pocket

Name

Date

■ Draw a line from 1 to 50 in order while saying each number.

What Is It?

■ Use the key below to color by number.

45 = orange   46 = yellow   47 = blue   48 = violet (purple)

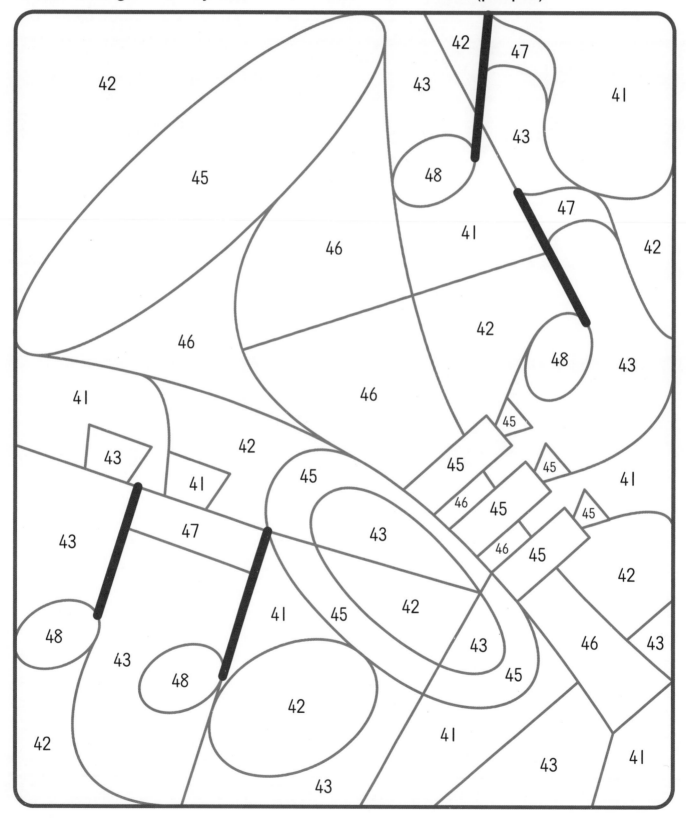

48

Sea Creatures

Name

Date

■ Draw a line from 1 to 50 in order while saying each number.

49

What Is It?

■ Use the key below to color by number.
47 = violet (purple)   48 = yellow   49 = orange   50 = red

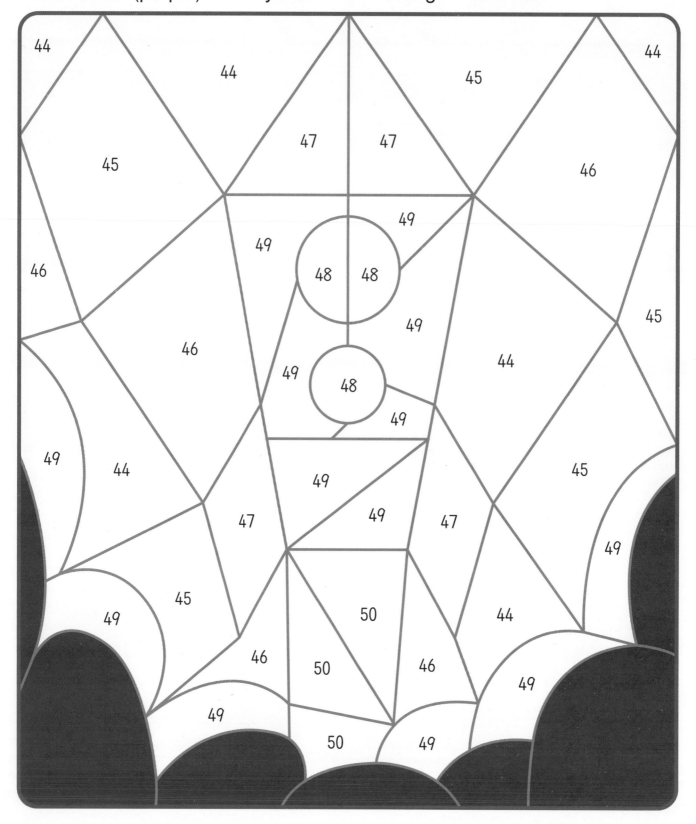

26 A Light under the Sea

Name

Date

■ Draw a line from 1 to 50 in order while saying each number.

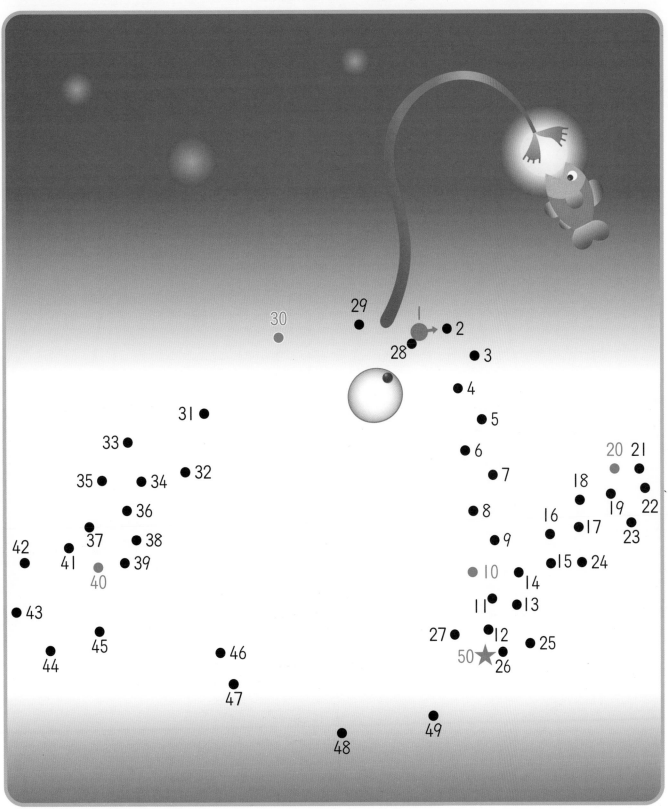

What Is It?

■ Use the key below to color by number.
41 = blue   43 = black   44 = green   47 = yellow

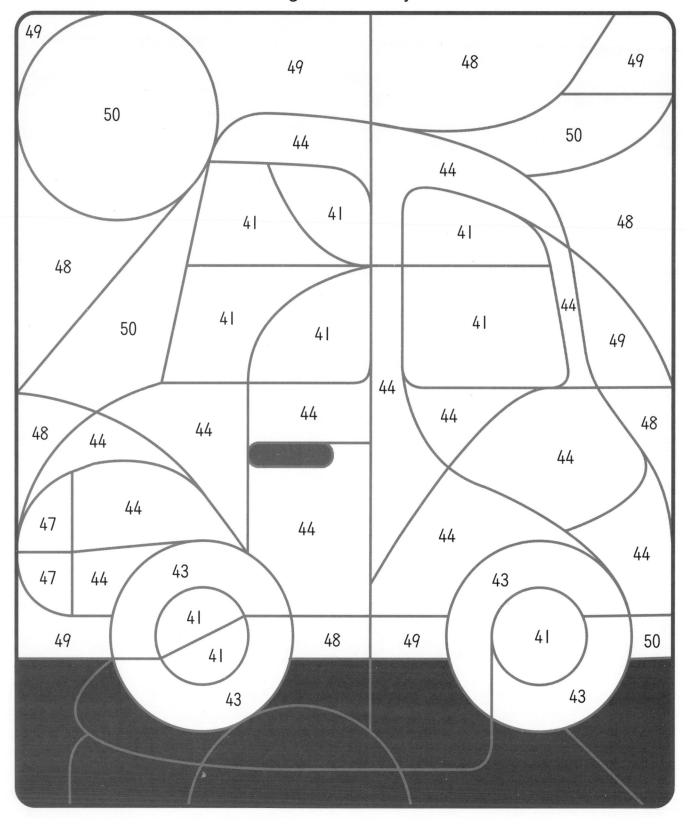

52

27 What Is on the Grass?

Name

Date

■ Draw a line from 1 to 50 in order while saying each number.

What Is It?

■ Use the key below to color by number.
42 = brown   45 = blue   46 = green   49 = yellow   50 = violet (purple)

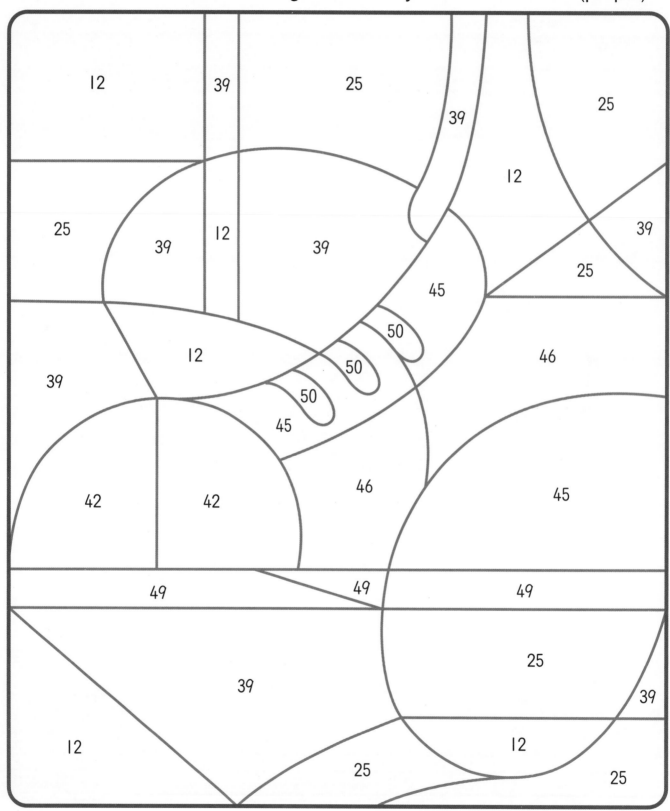

Have You Found Me?

Name

Date

To parents On this page, your child will have to draw many lines that cross other lines. If your child has difficulty finding the numbers, please point them out for him or her. Please praise your child as he or she finishes each activity.

■ Draw a line from 1 to 50 in order while saying each number.

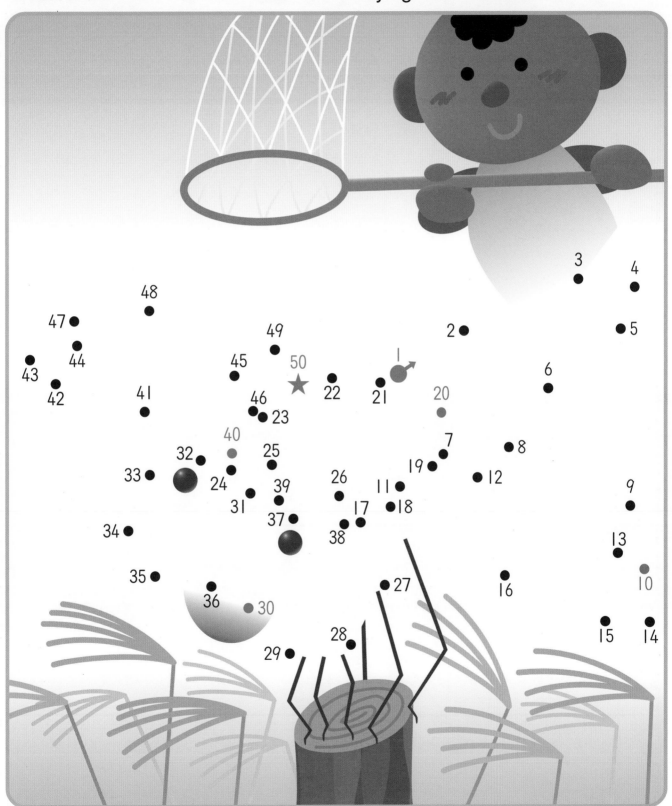

What Is It?

■ Use the key below to color by number.

41 = black   43 = blue   44 = yellow   47 = green   48 = violet (purple)

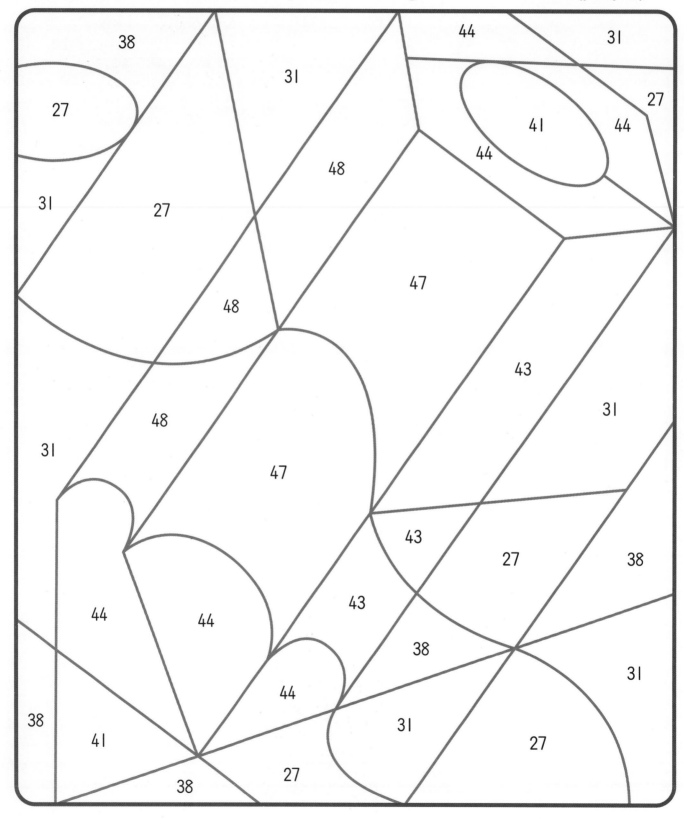

Ride 'em, Cowboy!

■ Draw a line from 1 to 50 in order while saying each number.

What Is It?

- Use the key below to color by number.
  42 = red   43 = blue   45 = black   49 = violet (purple)   50 = orange

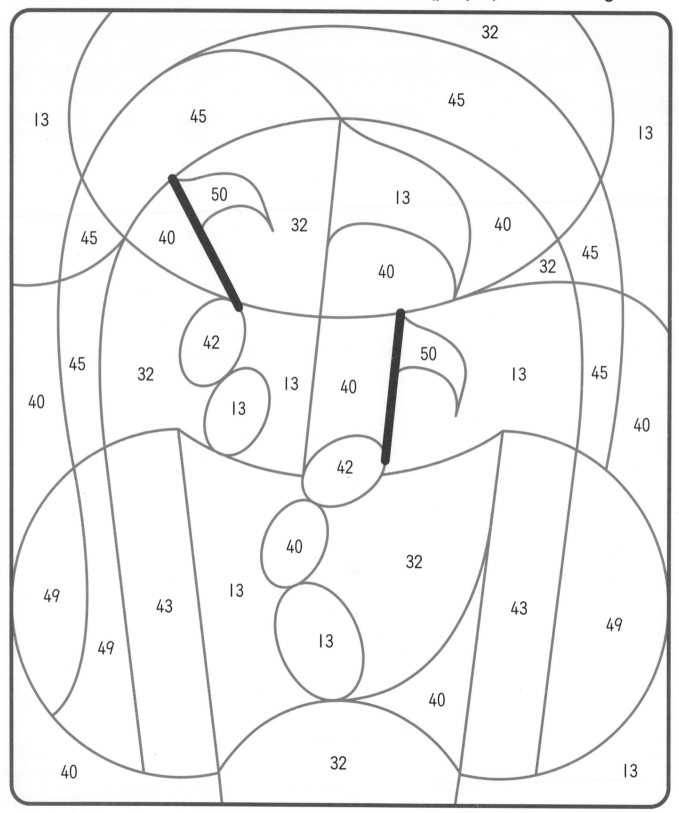

58

30 Flying at Night

Name

Date

■ Draw a line from 1 to 50 in order while saying each number.

What Is It?

■ Use the key below to color by number.
   41 = blue   42 = yellow   44 = violet (purple)   46 = brown   48 = green

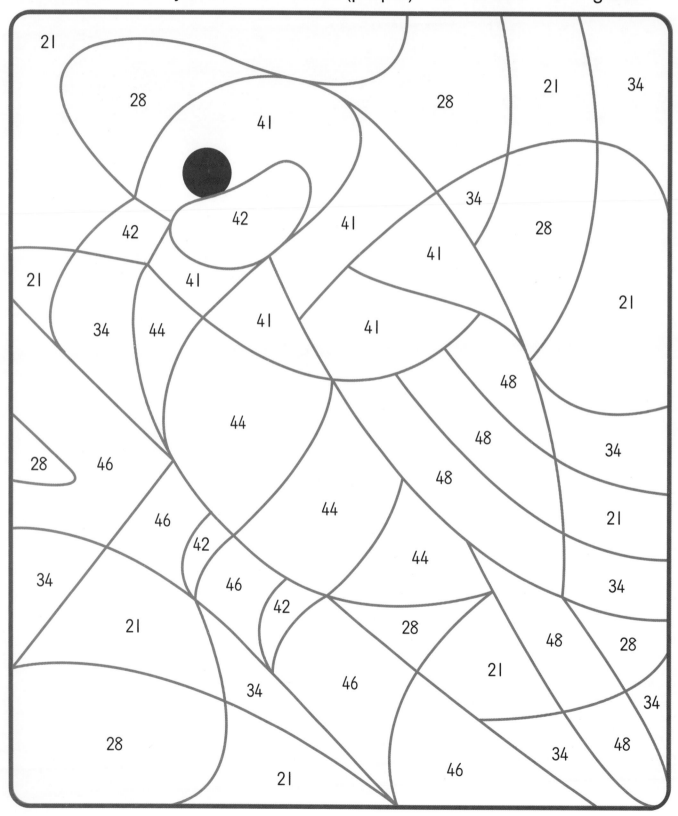

60

31

Look Out, Mouse!

Name

Date

■ Draw a line from 1 to 50 in order while saying each number.

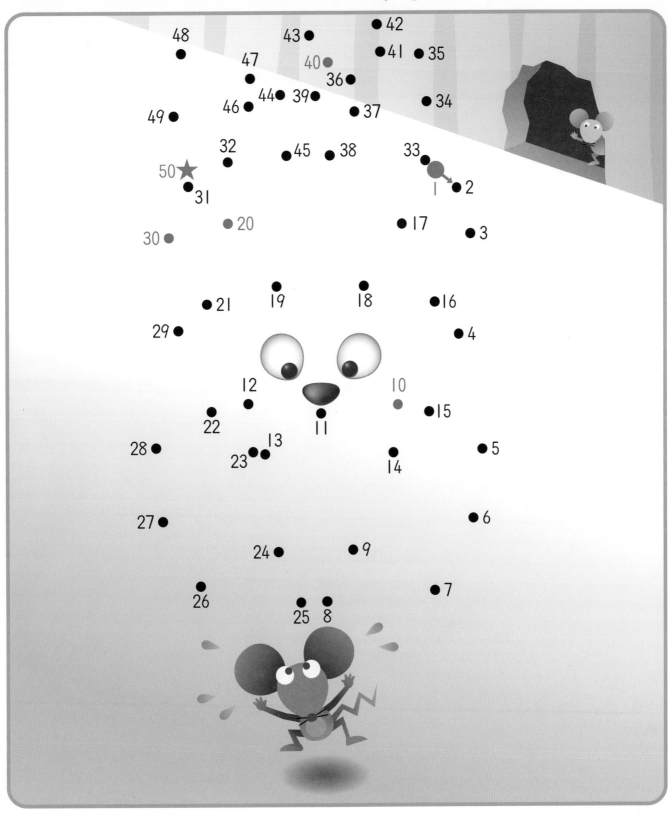

What Is It?

■ Use the key below to color by number.

43 = orange   45 = brown   47 = yellow   49 = red   50 = black

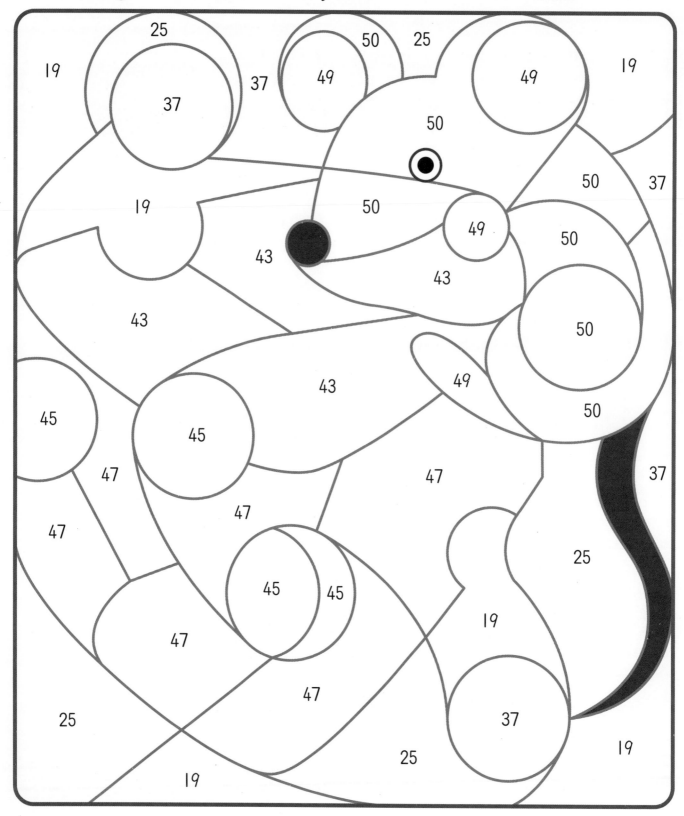

Ice Skating

32

Name

Date

■ Draw a line from 1 to 60 in order while saying each number.

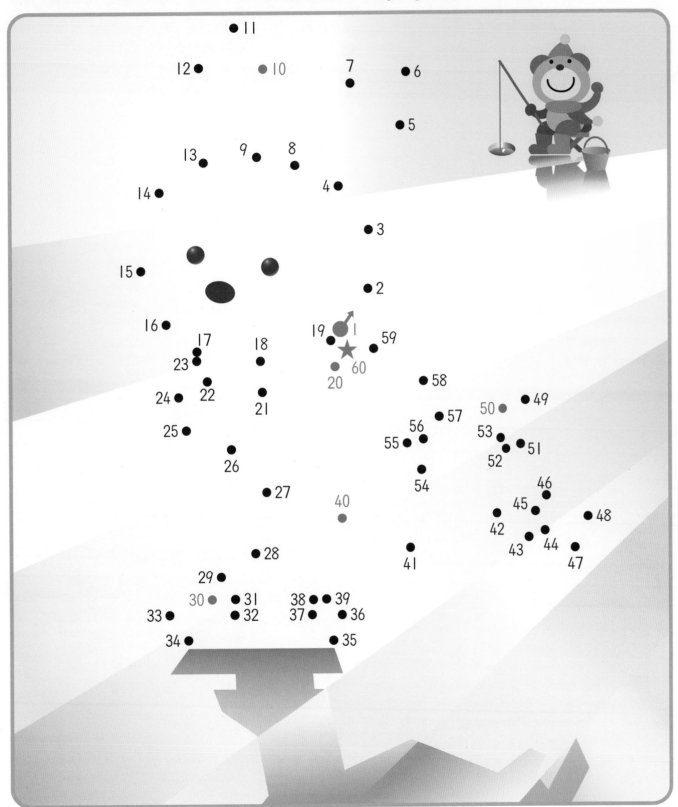

What Is It?

■ Use the key below to color by number.
 51 = black   52 = brown   53 = green   54 = red   55 = yellow

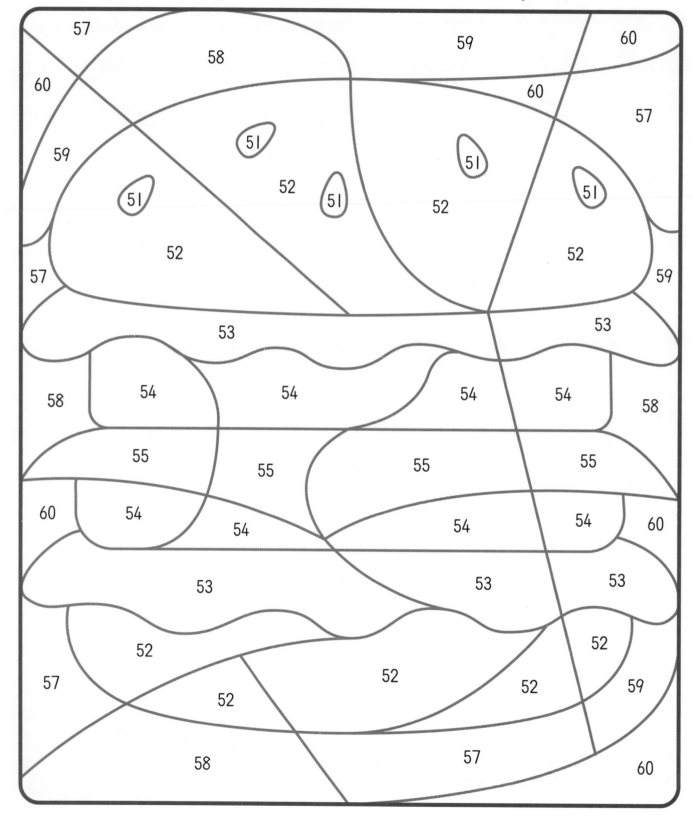

33

Can You Spot Me?

Name

Date

To parents Starting on page 65, the numbers become more difficult to find. If your child has difficulty finding the numbers, please point them out for him or her. Please praise your child as he or she finishes each activity.

■ Draw a line from 1 to 60 in order while saying each number.

What Is It?

■ Use the key below to color by number.

56 = green   57 = blue   58 = black   59 = yellow   60 = violet (purple)

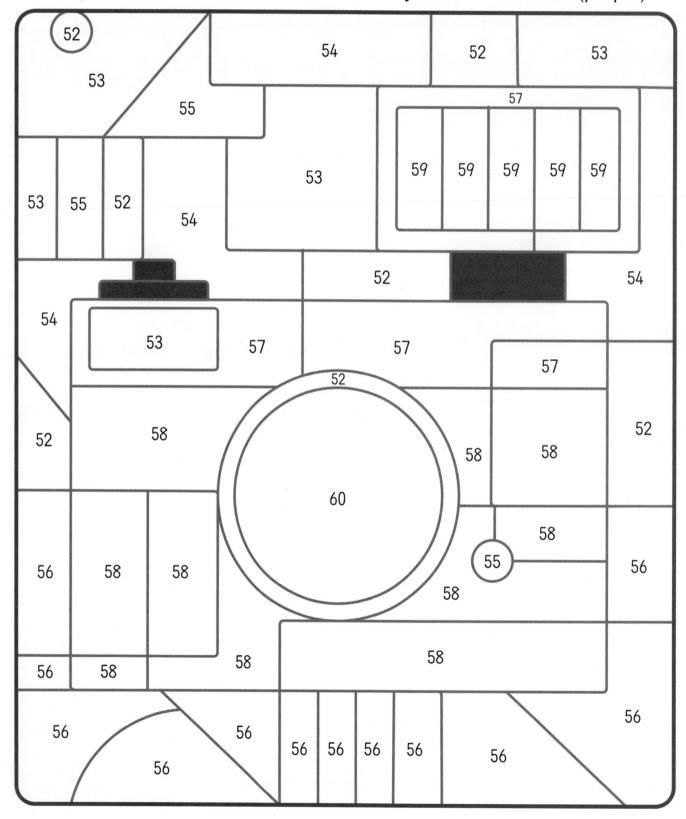

34 Congratulations!

Name

Date

■ Draw a line from 1 to 60 in order while saying each number.

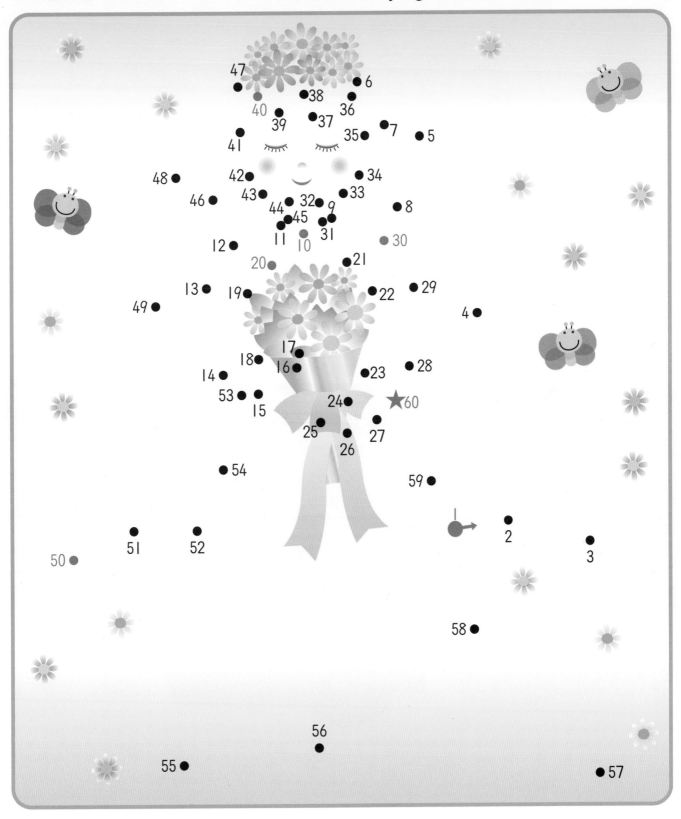

What Is It?

■ Use the key below to color by number.

52 = black   53 = orange   54 = yellow   55 = blue   58 = red   59 = green

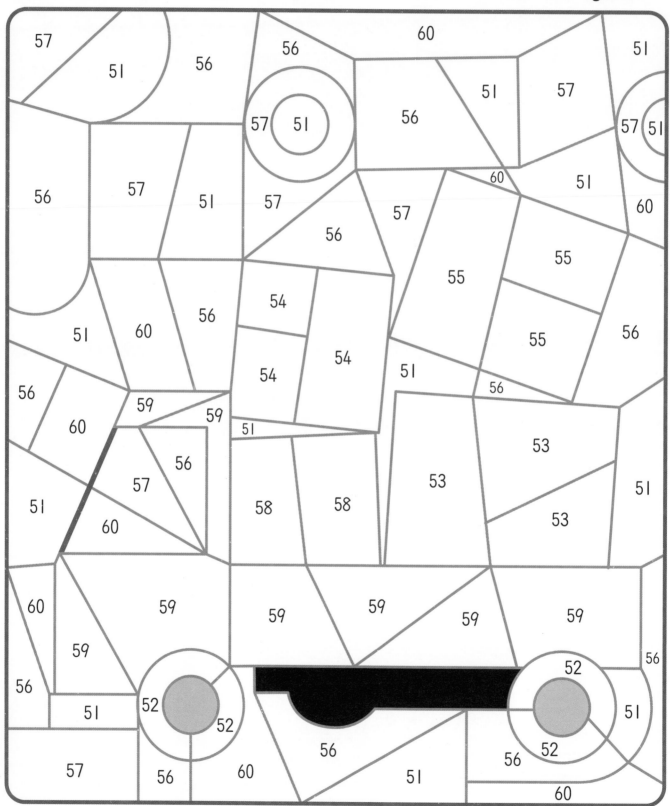

Eek! A Bug!

■ Draw a line from 1 to 70 in order while saying each number.

What Is It?

■ Use the key below to color by number.
61 = yellow 62 = red 63 = blue 64 = green 65 = orange 66 = brown

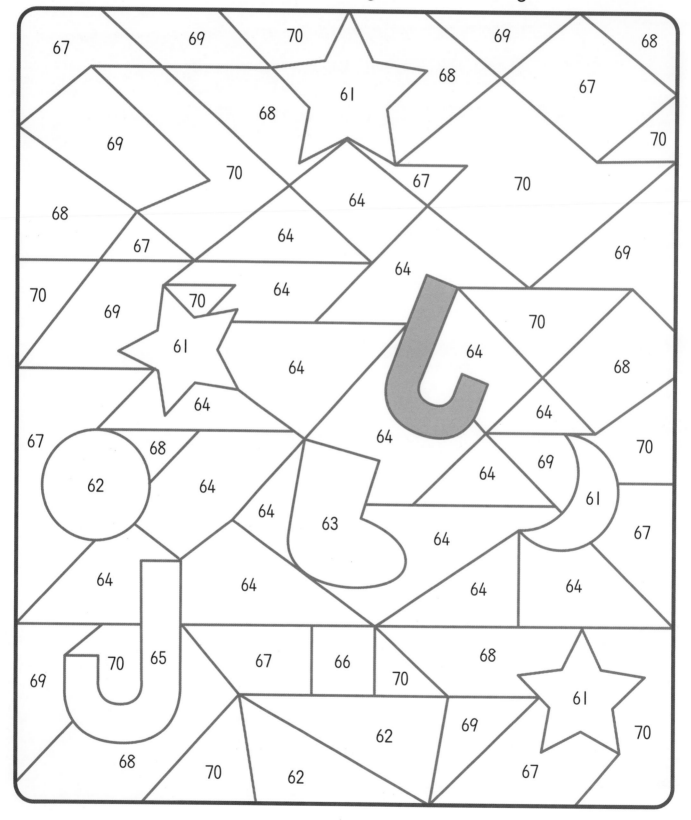

Help Me!

■ Draw a line from 1 to 70 in order while saying each number.

What Is It?

■ Use the key below to color by number.
  65 = red   66 = yellow   67 = blue   68 = green   69 = orange   70 = black

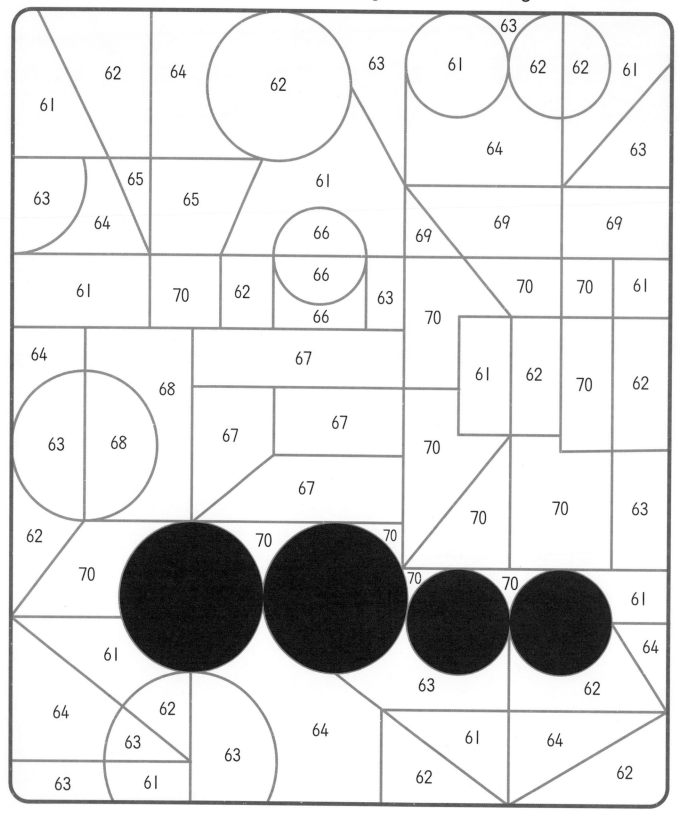

Oops!

Name

Date

■ Draw a line from 1 to 70 in order while saying each number.

73

What Is It?

■ Use the key below to color by number.
62 = blue   63 = red   64 = yellow   65 = black   66 = orange   68 = brown

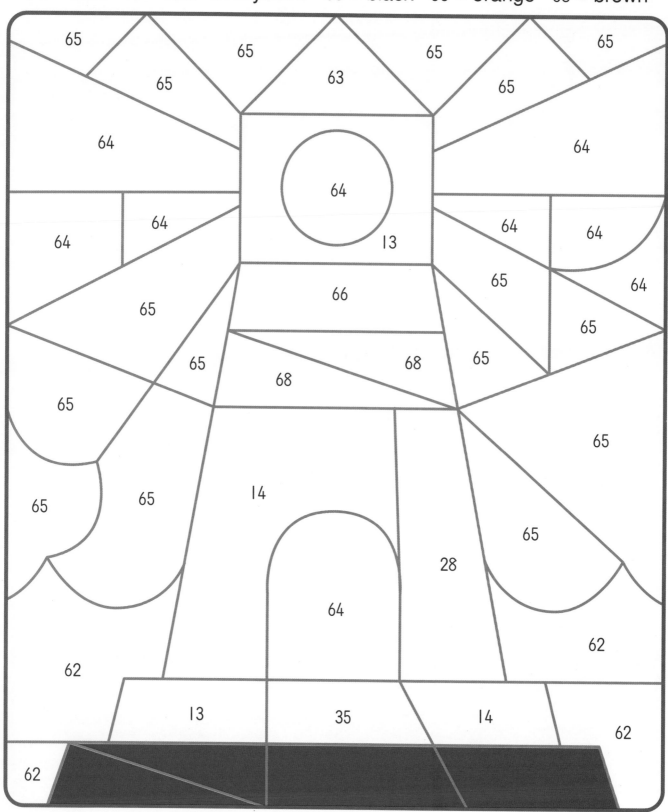

Who Is Juggling?

Name

Date

■ Draw a line from 1 to 70 in order while saying each number.

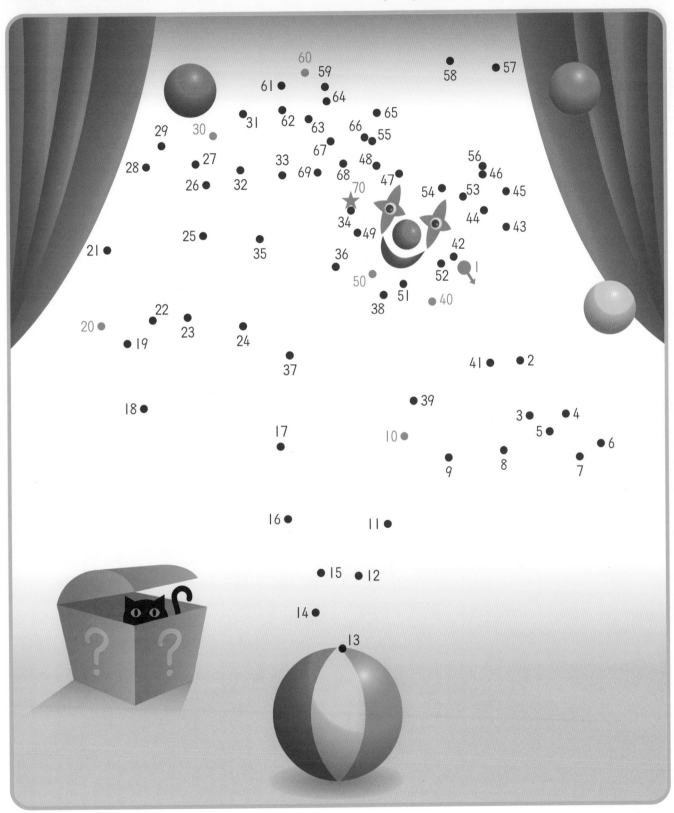

What Is It?

■ Use the key below to color by number.
61 = yellow   64 = orange   67 = red   68 = violet (purple)   69 = black   70 = blue

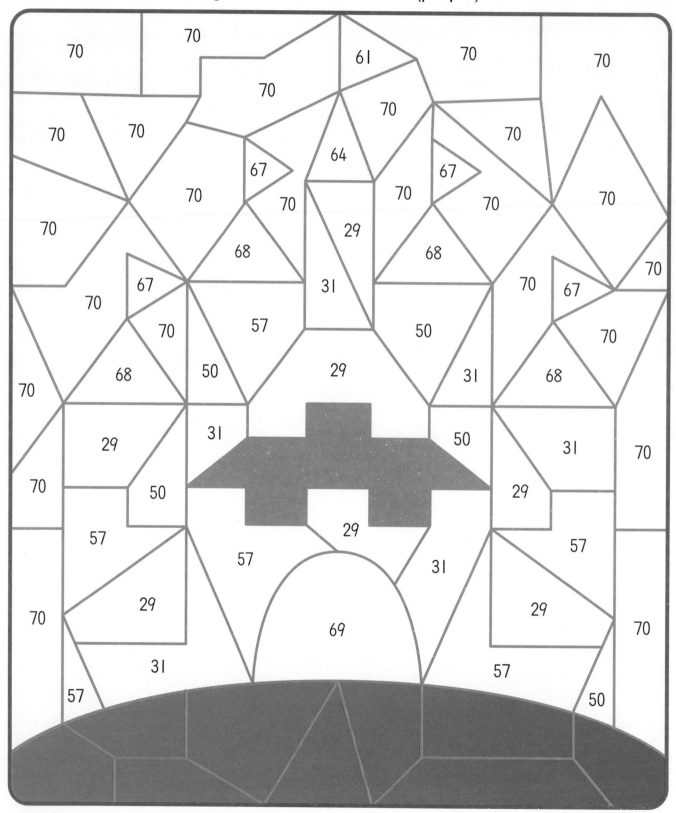

76

Answer Key

p.1 cake

p. 2 star

p. 3 doghouse

p. 4 ball

p. 5 hang glider

p. 6 green pepper

p. 7 lightning

p. 8 bunch of bananas

p. 9 paper airplane

p. 10 elephant

p. 11 tent

p. 12 flounder

p. 13 holiday tree

p. 14 hat

p. 15 snail

p. 16 football

p. 17 butterfly

p. 18 tree

p. 19 snake

p. 20 Stegosaurus

Answer Key

p. 21 mole

p. 22 tropical fish

p. 23 sea lion

p. 24 soft ice cream

p. 25 frog

p. 26 seal

p. 27 piano

p. 28 cap

p. 29 balloon

p. 30 magic lamp

p. 31 whale

p. 32 rose

p. 33 pig

p. 34 present

p. 35 wolf

p. 36 cake

p. 37 koala

p. 38 coat

p. 39 puffer fish

p. 40 cat

Answer Key

p. 41 elephant

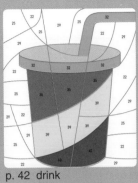

p. 42 drink

p. 43 hatching chick

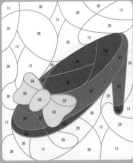

p. 44 high-heeled shoe

p. 45 hatching Tyrannosaurus

p. 46 helmet

p. 47 kangaroo

p. 48 trumpet

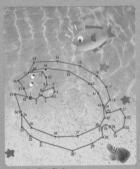

p. 49 flatfish

p. 50 rocket

p. 51 angler fish

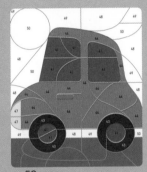

p. 52 car

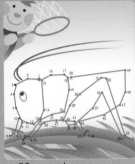

p. 53 grasshopper

p. 54 sneaker

p. 55 dragonfly

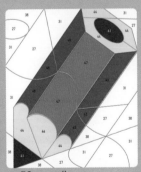

p. 56 pencil

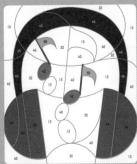

p. 57 horse

p. 58 headphones

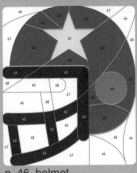

p. 59 bat

p. 60 bird

Answer Key

p. 61 cat

p. 62 mouse and cheese

p. 63 rabbit

p. 64 hamburger

p. 65 leopard

p. 66 camera

p. 67 bride

p. 68 truck

p. 69 praying mantis

p. 70 holiday tree

p. 71 bear

p. 72 train

p. 73 dog

p. 74 lighthouse

p. 75 clown

p. 76 castle

KUM☺N

Certificate of Achievement

is hereby congratulated on completing

My Book of Number Games 1 - 70

Presented on _____ , 20 ____

_____
Parent or Guardian

1   2   3   4
color-by-number